INSIGHT COMPACT GUIDES

ISRAEL

Compact Guide: Israel is the ideal guide to this dynamic land, taking you from the golden beaches of Tel Aviv and the golden domes of Jerusalem to the marvels of the Dead Sea and the playground of Eilat. Historical and cultural briefings augment the travel information.

This is one of almost 100 titles in *Insight Guides'* series of pocket-sized, easy-to-use guidebooks intended for the independent-minded traveller. *Compact Guides* are in essence travel encyclopedias in miniature, designed to be comprehensive yet portable, as well as up-to-date and authoritative.

GW00722609

Star Attractions

An instant reference to some of Israel's most popular tourist attractions to help you on your way.

Dome of the Rock p 22

Jerusalem's Western Wall p 23

Church of the Holy Sepulchre p 25

Via Dolorosa p 27

Bethlehem p 30

Tel Aviv p 33

Eilat p 38

Nazareth p 51

Festivals p 84

The Negev p 77

Israel

Introduction

Places

Culture

Leisure

Practical Information

watershed at an altitude of 800m (2,560ft). It takes only half a day to drive from the most northerly point on the Syrian-Lebanese border to the Red Sea. After skiing in the early morning on the slopes of Mount Hermon one can spend the afternoon gazing at tropical fish around the coral reefs of Eilat.

Water is one of the most important elements in the country, and the resolution of distribution problems has been an essential aspect of the peace negotiations. A contributory cause of the Six-Day War was Israel's determination to use its military supremacy to protect its access to the waters of the Jordan, which it claimed Syria planned to re-route. Today, 85 percent of the state's water reserves are provided by the occupied territories and much of the tension in the area results from discriminatory laws governing water extraction and use.

While most of the southern part of Israel is basically desert, in the Negev and the Arava Valley a pipeline system has been constructed to carry the water more than 300km (190 miles) from the Sea of Galilee to create vast plantations and lush green fields.

The latter form a marked contrast to the nearby Dead Sea, whose surface lies 392m (1,254ft) below sea level, making it the lowest point on the earth's surface. Since its waters do not drain away, they are extremely salty – so salty, in fact, that no life is possible, hence the name.

Economically speaking, the most important part of Israel is the coastal plain running along the Mediterranean. Here live three-quarters of the country's population, and here you will find three-quarters of the nation's industry. Half the agricultural output also stems from this region. The principal city here is Tel Aviv, the country's foremost trading centre situated between the twin ports of Haifa in the north and Ashdod in the south.

6

Peach harvesting

Making music, Jerusalem

Israel – The Holy Land

Framed by the Mediterranean, the River Jordan and the Dead Sea, and the setting of holy sites revered by three world religions, Israel has been for centuries a magnet for pilgrims and tourists. Here are the landscapes and locations where events described in the Bible actually took place. It was here that Abraham moved with his flocks to new pastures; it was here, too, that David fought and won against the Philistine giant Goliath, and Jesus and his disciples wandered across the hills of Galilee.

Orthodox Jew at prayer

It is an unforgettable experience to drive past fragrant orchards of lemon trees to the holy cities of Jerusalem, Bethlehem and Nazareth, to bathe from the sandy beaches of the Mediterranean or in the deep blue waters of the Red Sea – and to visit the historical ruins and bizarre rock formations of the Negev Desert.

But these are not the only possibilities that a visit to Israel has to offer. Young people can help bring in the orange harvest or take part in archaeological excavations. Nature-lovers can walk for days through unspoiled countryside. And those in search of improved health can take a cure in the Dead Sea.

Location and Landscape

Israel lies at the meeting point between three continents. Geographically it belongs to Asia, culturally to Europe and climatically to Africa. The western frontier is formed by the Mediterranean Sea. In the north, the country is bordered by Syria and Lebanon. In the east it shares a border with Jordan, and to the south lie Egypt and the Red Sea. After the Six-Day War of 1967 Israel occupied the Syrian Golan Heights, a 40-km (25-mile) strip of Lebanon and the region on the West Bank of the River Jordan which formerly belonged to Jordan. The Sinai Peninsula, which was conquered during the same war, was returned to Egypt in 1979 as part of the Camp David Agreement. In 1993, as agreed in the Gaza-Jericho Agreement, Israel withdrew from the Gaza Strip and the Jericho region, as well as Hebron and Bethlehem, in order to make way for the founding of a Palestinian state.

Boats at Nasholim

Without the occupied territories, Israel covers an area of only 20,000sq km (7,700sq miles) – in other words, it is about the same size as Massachusetts and slightly smaller than Wales. What it lacks in territory, however, it makes up in variety. Israel is a long, thin country. Running like a backbone from north to south are the mountains of Judaea, which divide the Great Rift Valley of the Jordan in the east from the flat coastal plain in the west. Jerusalem lies in the middle of the Judaean

5

Climate

From April until October the temperatures are warm and summery. Between the months of June and August it can become very hot, especially in the south. Winter, which is mild, occurs from November until March. Snow rarely falls in Jerusalem; if it does so, then mostly in January. It frequently rains during the winter months. After a wet period, however, the sun will often shine again for days on end. Summer reigns even in winter in Eilat. Good months to visit Israel are April and May, when the temperatures are spring-like and pleasant, the flowers are in bloom and the warmth of the sun permits bathing in the Mediterranean. Furthermore, during this season the hotels are not yet full of summer holidaymakers.

On the beach, Tel Aviv

Nature and environment

From the very beginning, Zionist settlers set about transforming the face of Palestine. The steppes were irrigated and the swamps were drained and, following the foundation of Israel in 1948, the 'Conquest of the Negev' was declared a national priority.

But there is a great deal of environmental awareness in Israel. A good example is the Emeq Hula (Hula Basin), which lies in the Jordan Valley north of the Sea of Galilee. Over thousands of years, vast marshlands and bogs had formed because the waters of the Jordan collected here on their way to the lake. When the State of Israel was formed, the marshland area covered some 65sq km (23sq miles). It was the home of more than 6,000 wild water buffaloes, countless wild boar, beavers, tortoises and the lynx-like wildcat. Then the farmers arrived, digging canals and planting eucalyptus trees in order to transform the Hula Basin into agricultural land.

7

A dolphin entertains at Eilat

In 1957 only 310ha (766 acres) of untouched swampland remained. In 1964, thanks to the efforts of conservationists, it was declared Israel's first nature conservancy area. Soon afterwards, a small herd of water buffaloes could be seen once more wallowing in the lakes; the species was placed under absolute protection. And once more papyrus can be found growing in clumps, and yellow water lilies fringe the shores. An observation tower and walkways of reed mats now allow the visitor to explore the Hula Basin in harmony with nature.

It was the enthusiasm of conservationists, too, which led the Knesset in 1963 to pass the law governing national parks and nature conservation areas and founding a Nature Protection Agency. Today, of Israel's total land area of only 21,000sqkm (8,100sq miles), some 3,000sqkm (1,100sq miles) have been designated as 311 separate protected areas. The SNPI (Society for the Protection of Nature in Israel) maintains visitors' and information centres

Kibbutz children, Nasholim

Ibex, Makhtesh Ramon Crater

at four of the most outstanding ones: at Arad, the 'Gateway to the Wilderness of Judea', in Mitzpe Ramon, on the edge of the Makhtesh Ramon, the largest crater area in the Negev, in Yotvata, a kibbutz in the southern Arava Valley which is responsible for the 'Biblical Zoo' Hai Bar, and in the Hule Basin in the north Jordan area.

The Hule National Park and the neighbouring reservations, Tel Dan, Banias and Ayoun, demonstrate the significance of such protected and unspoiled habitats for the world's ecology. Every year, tens of thousands of storks cross a narrow strip of the Jordan valley, only a few kilometres wide. Cranes follow the same route, and hordes of pink pelicans from the Danube delta regularly spend several days here on their migrations to and from Africa. Fish, however, are the most important creatures here: more than 500 different species live along the Mediterranean coast, in the Sea of Galilee and in the Red Sea.

Population

The Jewish population of Israel is rising rapidly, mainly because of immigration. The Israeli heartland has a population of 5.9 million. Some 4.7 million of these are Jews, whilst the rest are Arabs. Some 870,000 Israelis are Muslims; 190,000 are Christians and 100,000 are Druzes. Under Israeli control, the Gaza Strip and the West Bank mixed 100,000 Jewish settlers with 2 million Palestinians.

Busy Ben Yehuda Street

Judaism

According to the regulations governing the Law of Return, all Jews have the right to make their home in Israel. When the state was founded in 1948, Israel had a population of approximately 650,000. Inspired by the political ideas of Zionism (the political movement for the establishment of a Jewish state in Palestine), they or their parents had arrived between 1882 and 1948 during one of the six main waves of immigration (Hebrew: *Aliya*), for until the mid-19th century fewer than 10,000 Jews lived in the Holy Land – most of them in Jerusalem.

The biggest *Aliya* began in 1948. Within a period of only three years, until 1951, almost 700,000 Jews from all over the world settled in Israel. During the following decades another million arrived, and during the early 1990s, following the collapse of the Eastern bloc, Israel took in another 800,000 Jews from Eastern European countries. More than half of today's population, however, are *Sabras*, in other words natives of Israel, and some 15 percent are second-generation Israelis. In total, 81 out of every 100 citizens profess the Jewish faith.

Judaism is the oldest of the world's three monotheistic religions. It is based on the Torah (the Five Books of Moses) and the Talmud ('Doctrine'), a collection of var-

Blowing the 'shofar' for the New Year

Holy Sepulchre Church

ious writings containing rules and interpretations which acquired its final form in the 5th century AD. Written in Hebrew, the language of Canaan, it contains the history of the Jewish people, the laws governing social life and the basic principles of the faith.

To hold a Jewish service in a synagogue, at least 10 male Jews must be present. During the service, men and women sit separately. Their heads must be covered. In contrast to Christianity, the Jewish religion does not recognise priests as intermediaries between God and the faithful. Rabbis are simply teachers characterised by their knowledge of the Torah and the Talmud. The highest religious authority in Israel is the orthodox Supreme Rabbinical Assembly, which ensures that the secular laws remain in harmony with the Torah. Orthodox Jews demand even more: if they had their way, the Torah itself would become the national constitution. Failing this, some refuse to recognise the state of Israel. They do no military service and live according to the laws of the Talmud in their own districts, such as the Mea She'arim quarter in Jerusalem.

The Western Wall

9

Islam

Islam is Israel's second most important religion, followed by approximately 15 percent of the population (other minority groups include Christians (2.5 percent) and Druze and others (1.7 percent). Its historical roots lie in Judaism as well as Christianity; the Old Testament fathers, like Jesus, are considered to be prophets. The last and most important prophet was Mohammed, who from the year 610 had God's revelations written down in the Koran.

The five basic duties of a Muslim are as follows: the belief in a single God (Allah) and in His prophet Mohammed, the repetition of prayers five times each day in the direction of Mecca, the giving of alms, the act of fasting during the month of Ramadan and the pilgrimage to Mecca

Muslim reading the Koran

Christianity

Christians have regarded Jerusalem with some ambivalence since Jesus was tried and crucified here. However, most sects are represented, from Roman Catholics to the many Protestant churches such as Greek Orthodox, the Armenians and the Copts. A priority has always been maintaining access to the holy places.

Languages

The official languages are modern Hebrew (*Ivrit*) and Arabic. Most Israelis also speak English and many of them remain fluent in the language of their country of origin. Yiddish, as a mixture of German and Hebrew, is still used worldwide as an international Jewish lingua franca, in particular as it can boast an extensive tradition of songs and other texts. There is often a lack of consistency in the transcription of geographical and proper names into Latin characters. Thus the town of Safed may also be written Saphet, Zephat, Tsefad, Zeat, Zfet and Sfad.

Bilingual direction sign, Jaffa Visitor Centre

Economy

Traditionally, agriculture has been one of the mainstays of the Israeli economy, which has a GNP of some US$42.6 billion, although less than one-quarter of the total land area is suitable for cultivation and less than 10 percent can be irrigated. Nonetheless, the Israeli government has always ascribed great importance to agriculture, not least for ideological reasons. One of the declared national goals is to make of the 'Land of our Fathers' an independent 'Home for the Jewish People'. That this should have been possible was partly due to the fact that the Zionist Jewish National Fund in Palestine, when it was under British and Turkish rule, acquired large areas of land from Arab landowners for Jewish immigrants. After 1948 this same organisation was responsible for the development of all land. Since, according to Old Testament principles, all land should remain common property, collective forms of settlement arose such as *kibbutzim* and *moshavim* (collective villages without and with private land ownership). To this day, almost all the land remains in public ownership.

Agriculture in Israel is capital-intensive. Thanks to massive state subsidies under the aegis of official and semi-official bodies such as the Jewish Agency, Israeli farmers produce some three-quarters of the country's requirements with the efforts of only 5 percent of the labour force. Furthermore, the export of agricultural products (especially citrus fruits) balances 10 percent of the import bill.

Israel, however, is not an agrarian state. On the contrary: even the 250 kibbutzim still in existence achieve most of their turnover through the manufacture and marketing of industrial products. Israel's textiles enjoy a high

Tomato harvesting on a kibbutz

Advanced industry: testing aerodynamics in a wind tunnel

reputation, as does its clothing industry, the production of leather goods and fur processing. Of even more importance is the industry in diamonds and precious stones, which employs some 30,000 people. Israel imports the uncut stones and re-exports them as valuable jewels. Every third diamond which is sold today comes from Israel. Thanks to the wealth of natural resources in and around the Dead Sea, the country is also an important manufacturer of chemical substances and large quantities of fertilisers. Not least, the external political situation and the high technical standards achieved by the Israeli education system have resulted in the country becoming a major manufacturer and exporter of weapons.

Tourism has long been an important sector of the economy, with around 2 million visitors arriving in the country every year. Partly as a result of increasing stability and opportunities brought about by the peace process, this figure is expected to rise in the coming years. Such stability would also make Israel less dependent on American aid, initiated in the 1970s when Israel was perceived to be an important military ally against the Soviet Union and which has sometimes exceeded $3 billion a year.

The State Seal, Knesset building

11

Politics and administration

Israel is a parliamentary democracy. Every four years the prime minister is elected directly, the government according to a system of proportional representation. The entire country forms a single constituency.

Parliament in session

Three political groups contest the 120 seats in the Knesset. All three existed as socio-political movements long before the state was formed and they represent widely varying approaches to the form the state should take. In no other parliament in the world are discussions as vehement and emotional as they are in the Knesset.

For the first three decades of the state's existence, the left-wing workers' parties which controlled government were closer to the Ashkenazi tradition and were modelled on the democracies of Europe. The immigration waves during the 1960s brought mostly Oriental Jews to Israel and resulted in a change of political balance. Regardless of their theoretical goals, the ruling Labour Parties had developed into representatives of the Euro-American Establishment, in which there was little room for the Oriental Jews. During the Anti-Establishment elections of 1977, the majority of Sephardic Jews therefore voted for the nationalist-conservative Likud bloc.

Sabbath costume of the Yemenite Jews

Since the founding of the state the various religious parties in Israel have attracted up to 15 percent of the votes. Their vociferous supporters advocate goals which range from the total rejection of the State of Israel to politico-religious chauvinism. Since no party has ever won an over-

all majority, Israel has always had coalition government and the complex alliances formed have usually ensured that the Knesset remains a hothouse of intrigue. Until 1968 the Mapai party, led by David Ben-Gurion and Levi Eshkol, dominated politics. It then merged with other groups to form the Labour party, which held power until 1977 under Golda Meir and Yitzhak Rabin. The right-wing Likud bloc then came to power under Menachem Begin, followed in 1983 by Yitzhak Shamir.

Following its electoral victory in 1977, Likud attempted in a controversial settlement policy to incorporate the occupied territories into a 'Greater Israel' – Eretz Israel – as the Biblical provinces of Judea and Samaria.

From 1984 to 1992 coalitions were led by Labour's Shimon Peres and Likud's Shamir. In 1992 a left-of-centre coalition led by Labour won the election, with Yitzhak Rabin returning as prime minister. Rabin was assassinated by a young Orthodox Jew in 1995. In the elections the following year the Likud bloc emerged victorious. The Likud, under prime minister Benjamin ('Bibi') Netanyahu, relies on the support of Orthodox factions in parliament.

12

The Palestinian Question

'We have nothing but this country!' – with this sentence the Palestinian writer Emile Habibi ended his speech in Jerusalem in 1992 when he became the first Israeli Arab to be awarded the prestigious Israeli Prize for Literature. He was well aware that by doing so he was borrowing the much-quoted Jewish claim to the very same country.

Habibi provides a good example of the many different parts played across the centuries by the Arab people known as the Palestinians. For many centuries Palestine was part of the Ottoman Empire, until in 1917 it was conquered by the British under Major Allenby and placed under British Mandate. In 1947 the United Nations decided to divide Palestine following the withdrawal of the British. This decree paved the way for the proclamation of the State of Israel on 14 May 1948, but led immediately to the first Arab-Israeli War. The end of hostilities was marked during the summer of 1949 by an armistice agreement between Israel and its four Arab neighbours which removed Palestine from the map.

According to the United Nations proposals, the end of the British mandate on 14 May 1948 should have led to the establishment of a single state of Palestine. This was to be an economic union between a Jewish and an Arab state with Jerusalem as an international zone. Instead of this, Israel was established on the land which historically had previously belonged to Palestine. The West Bank, which Israel had not conquered during the 1948–9 war, was incorporated into Jordan. Egypt placed the Gaza Strip

under its own military authority. Since this date, Palestine has existed only as a geographical expression for the land between the Mediterranean Sea and the River Jordan.

In 1950 the United Nations registered 960,000 Palestinian refugees who had been driven out of Israel during the war or who had fled to neighbouring Arab countries, especially the Gaza Strip and the West Bank, where they were living in camps. About 170,000 Palestinian Arabs continued to live in the Israeli heartland.

The Palestinians who remained in Israel and their children now total 800,000 and have Israeli passports. The 900,000 or so Palestinians on the West Bank are technically Jordanian citizens. The 700,000 or so who inhabit the Gaza Strip were formally stateless. Both groups could apply for United Nations Refugee passports.

Postcards with attitude

Through the foundation of the Palestine Liberation Organisation (PLO) in 1964, which carried out terrorist attacks on Israel, the Palestinian people created a national representational body, which was especially effective after the election of Yasser Arafat as its chairman.

When, on 1 August 1988, King Hussein officially ceded Jordan's sovereignty over the West Bank to the Palestinians, the latter proclaimed on 15 November 1988 in Algiers their own state on the land west of the Jordan and the Gaza Strip, a region which Israel at that stage refused to abandon. The Palestinians' policy of civil disobedience in the occupied territories, together with a great deal of external political pressure, ultimately resulted in the matter being brought to the negotiating table.

13

Following the Gaza-Jericho Agreement of 1993 in Washington and the agreements negotiated in Cairo in 1994 between the PLO and Israel to ensure its execution, the Palestinians are in possession of self-governed autonomous regions for the first time in their history.

A checkpoint chat

Historical Highlights

c2000BC Migration of Semitic peoples from Mesopotamia to Palestine. According to the Bible they are led by Abraham into Canaan, God's 'Promised Land'.

c1700BC Abraham's nomadic successors leave Canaan and reach Egypt. Biblical sources relate that Jacob's son Joseph becomes viceroy.

c1480BC The pharaoh Tutmosis III makes Palestine an Egyptian province.

c1300BC Under the leadership of Moses and his brother Aaron, the 'Children of Israel' journey from Egypt back to Palestine.

c1200BC The Philistines from the Aegean region advance north along the Mediterranean coast of Palestine. They are stopped by Pharaoh Ramses III near Port Said and settle in Palestine.

c1000BC Under King Saul, the Israelites are defeated by the Philistines near Gilboa. Saul's successor, David, defeats the Philistine Goliath in a legendary duel and conquers Jerusalem, which he makes his capital.

960–925BC During the reign of King Solomon, David's son, the First Temple in Jerusalem is built. After Solomon's death, the Kingdom of the Israelites disintegrates into two halves: Israel in the north and Judah in the south.

745–727BC Under Tiglatpilesar III, the Assyrian Empire destroys the Kingdom of Israel and subjugates the Kingdom of Judah.

587–538BC King Nebuchadnezzar of Babylon razes Jerusalem and leads its citizens into captivity in Babylon. After his death in 562BC his kingdom disintegrates and Palestine becomes a Persian province. In 538 King Cyrus ends the exile of the Israelites. They return to Jerusalem and erect the Second Temple.

336–323BC Alexander the Great destroys the Persian empire.

200BC Palestine is conquered by Alexander's successors, the Seleucids, who leave behind an unmistakable Greek stamp on the country.

169BC A Jewish uprising under the Maccabees protests at the Hellenisation of the country.

64BC The country becomes a Roman province under Pompey the Great.

39–4BC Under the protection of Rome, Herod the Great becomes king of Palestine. He has the Second Temple in Jerusalem extended, founds the port of Caesarea in honour of the Emperor Augustus and fortifies Masada.

4BC–40AD His son, Herod Antipas, rules Palestine on behalf of Rome. According to the New Testament account, Jesus of Nazareth was crucified under the Roman governor Pontius Pilate (26BC–AD36) in approximately AD33.

66–135AD Repeated Jewish uprisings against Rome. In AD70 the Emperor Titus destroys Jerusalem and the Second Temple. In 135 the Emperor Hadrian ends the last major revolt under Bar Kochba, denies the Jews access to Jerusalem and transforms the city into the Roman military colony of Aelia Capitolina.

306–337 The Roman emperor Constantine recognises Christianity as an equal religion.

396 Following the division of the Roman Empire, Palestine falls under the jurisdiction of Constantinople (Byzantium). Virtually no Jews are left in Palestine.

638 Palestine is conquered by Omar, the Second Caliph and successor of Mohammed. Following Arab immigration waves, Palestine becomes increasingly Islamic.

1095 Pope Urban II calls for the 'Liberation of the Holy Land from the Heathen'. This marks the beginning of the crusades.

1099 Jerusalem falls to the Christian armies, who slaughter many of the city's inhabitants. The crusaders christen the conquered area of Palestine the 'Kingdom of Jerusalem'. Their greatest opponent on the Islamic side is Saladin.

1291 The Age of Crusades is over. In 1244 Jerusalem falls and by 1271 almost the whole of Palestine is in the hands of Sultan Beibar. In 1291 Acco falls, the last bastion of Christianity in the Holy Land. The Arab Mamelukes from Egypt rule Palestine, which is almost deserted.

1516 The Turks conquer Palestine. During the reign of Sultan Suleiman the Magnificent (1520–66) it experiences a Golden Age. Then it sinks back into insignificance under the Turks.

1897 Dr Theodor Herzl founds the Zionist World Congress in Basle with the declared aim of founding a Jewish state.

1917 Zionism claims its first major victory when Britain promises Jews a 'National Home' for the Jewish people in Palestine as part of the Balfour Declaration. British troops move into Palestine.

1920 The League of Nations grants Britain a mandate over Palestine. During the next decades increasing numbers of Jews migrate to Palestine. The Arabs living in the country protest in vain.

1939 Britain attempts to stop the immigration, but in view of the Nazi persecution of Jews, is not supported by the rest of the world.

1947 Despite Arab protests, the United Nations backs a British proposal to grant the Jews their own state in Palestine. Palestine is to be divided into a Jewish and an Arab state, with Jerusalem as an international zone.

1948 The British mandate ends on 14 May, and David Ben-Gurion proclaims the State of Israel. The new country is recognised by the USA and the USSR. During the subsequent 'War of Independence' Israel not only withstands the armies of the Arab League but also acquires considerably more land within Palestine than the UN had envisaged. This laid the basis for conflict.

1956–7 Israel leads the Sinai Offensive against Egypt but is forced by the UN to withdraw.

1967 Faced with the threats of the Arab nations and attacks by the Palestine Liberation Organisation (PLO), Israel occupies during the Six-Day War all Jordanian territory west of the Jordan, the Egyptian Sinai Peninsula and the Syrian Golan Heights. Ignoring UN protests, Israel refuses to withdraw, so that 2 million Arabs now live on territory occupied by Israeli armed forces.

1973 Egypt, Syria and Jordan attempt to reconquer the land lost to Israel during the Yom Kippur War, named after the day on which the offensive started. No territory changes hands. Israel begins to establish settlements in the occupied territories, where the PLO claims to be the legitimate representative of the Palestinians.

1977–9 In November 1977 the president of Egypt, Anwar Sadat, pays an official visit to Jerusalem. On 26 March 1979 the Camp David Agreement is signed in Washington. Israel subsequently withdraws from the Sinai Peninsula.

1980 The 'Jerusalem Law' reaffirms Israeli sovereignty over East Jerusalem.

1987 The Intifada begins: Palestinians in the occupied West Bank region and the Gaza Strip institute a campaign of civil disobedience and riots.

1990–1 The Iraqi annexation of Kuwait and the arrival of Eastern European Jews in Israel and the Occupied Territories force the US in particular to seek a solution to the Middle East conflict.

1992 The Labour Party under Yitzhak Rabin replaces the conservative Likud as the ruling party.

1993 Following negotiations between Israel and the PLO under Yasser Arafat, the Gaza-Jericho Agreement is signed in Washington. This places the Gaza Strip and Jericho environs under independent Palestinian administration.

1994 After 27 years in exile, Yasser Arafat officially enters the Gaza Strip. He declares Jericho the administrative capital. The militant Palestinian faction Hamas stages attacks to kill the peace process. A peace treaty is agreed in Washington between Israel and Jordan.

1995 On 4 November prime minister Yitzak Rabin is shot at a peace rally in Tel Aviv by a young Orthodox Jew. His successor, Simon Peres, vows to continue the peace process.

1996 Continued bombings by Hamas make the peace process more difficult. Likud leader Benjamin Netanyahu wins June elections.

1997–8 Further terror attacks as well as expansion of Jewish settlements bring peace negotiations temporarily to a halt.

Spring at the Tower of David

Preceding pages: Jerusalem and the Dome of Rock

A medieval view of Solomon and Sheba

Route 1

★★★ Jerusalem – the threefold Holy City

The Hebrew name 'Yerushalayim' means 'The Place of Peace'; the Arabic, 'El Kuds' means 'The Holy One'. For the faithful of three world religions, Jews, Christians and Muslims alike, Jerusalem is a holy city. 'Pray for the peace of Jerusalem!' announces the Psalmist in the 122nd Psalm. 'Peace be within thy walls, and prosperity within thy palaces. For my brethren and companions' sakes, I will now say, Peace be within thee.' The 3,000th anniversary of the city's foundation was celebrated in 1996 with no pains spared, and the longing for lasting peace remains as fervent as ever.

History

According to the Biblical account, King Solomon, the son of King David, built a temple for the province on the rocky plateau of Moria in about 960BC. This First Temple was destroyed by King Nebuchadnezzar of Babylon in 587BC. At some point after 520BC the plateau was enlarged by rocky infill for the new temple built under Nehemiah after the return from captivity in Babylon. This second temple stood for more than 500 years, until Herod the Great (37–4BC) undertook a complete renovation, enlarging the Temple Mount once again and surrounding it with supporting walls to contain the infill.

It was on the Temple Mount of Herod's day, which occupies about one-sixth of the Old Town, that the events described in the New Testament took place, amongst them the banishment of the money changers from the temple. The most sacred monument of Judaism was completely destroyed in 70AD by Emperor Titus. Since that time there has been no Jewish temple on the mount. Pious Jews avoid the place in order not to step inadvertently on the spot which was once reserved for high priests of the faith. Jerusalem's magnificence during Roman times and the dominant location of the temple on the Temple Mount within the city itself can be appreciated by studying a model of Jerusalem which was built in 1969 by the Israeli archaeologist Avi Yonah to a scale of 1:50 (situated in the garden of the Holyland Hotel, Bayit Gan, West Jerusalem; daily 8am–4pm).

Model of ancient Jerusalem at the Holyland Hotel

In 638 the Muslims conquered the city, declared the Temple Mount to be an Islamic holy place and built over the next century two of their most important mosques on the rocky plateau.

Thereafter, for almost 150 years, from 1099 until 1244, Jerusalem was ruled by the European Crusaders. The Old Town owes them most of the accepted localisations of Biblical events. The Crusaders mostly built a church or chapel to mark the spot, or in some cases extended an existing place of worship. They were driven out of Palestine by the Egyptian Mamelukes, who in their turn lost command over the city (and indeed of the entire country) to the Turkish Sultan Selim I in 1517. His son, Suleiman, became the greatest builder Jerusalem has ever known.

19

During the 19th century Jerusalem expanded far beyond the walls of the Old Town. New residential districts grew up particularly in the west and north. By the end of the century, the city had 50,000 inhabitants comprising approximately equal numbers of Jews, Muslims and Christians.

On 11 December 1917 the British army under General Allenby entered Jerusalem. Three years later the city became the headquarters of the British High Commission for the whole of Palestine. When the British left the country on 14 May 1948, fighting began between Israelis and Jordanians, during the course of which neither side was able to conquer the city for itself. Following the armistice agreement in the spring of 1949, the newer West Jerusalem belonged to Israel and East Jerusalem including the Old City to Jordan. The city was divided by an impassable demarcation line. The only way across was via the Almond Tree Gate (known today as Kikar Piqud HaMerkaz), which lay to the northeast of the Old City, where foreigners but neither Jews nor Arabs could cross from one part of the city to the other under UN supervision.

Independence day celebrations at the Western Wall

In June 1967 Israel conquered East Jerusalem and began at once to implement building projects to remove all evidence of the divided city. In 1980 the conservative Likud government promulgated a law that 'the entire and unified Jerusalem is in its entirety the eternal capital of Israel'. This uncompromising claim continues to be refuted by the United Nations as well as by almost every nation

The Muslim Quarter

in the world. For this reason, virtually all foreign embassies are in Tel Aviv. Since 1980, however, Israel has continued to build Jewish residential complexes in the eastern part of the city, which is inhabited mainly by Arabs.

Sights

The great holy shrines of the three world religions: the Western Wall, the Church of the Holy Sepulchre, the Dome of the Rock and the al-Aqsa Mosque, the most important historical sites and the most atmospheric bazaar – in other words, the main attractions which tourists want to see when they visit Jerusalem – form a part of East Jerusalem, the section of the city annexed by Israel in 1967. West Jerusalem, which until 1967 formed the capital of Israel, houses the sites which were constructed after the founding of the state of Israel: the Knesset, the Israel Museum, the

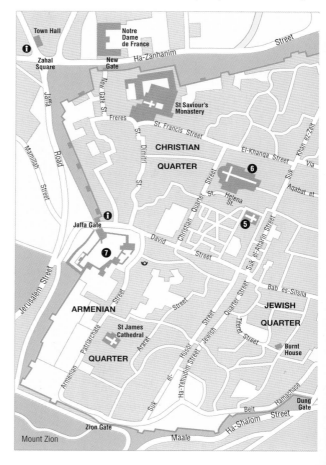

Yad Vashem and the Hadassah Hospital with its 12 windows by Chagall. East of the Old City, on the far side of the Kidron Valley, lies the Mount of Olives, which is some 100m (320ft) high and which can best be approached on foot through the so-called Gate of Gethsemane.

Plaque in the Garden of Gethsemane

The Old City

Jerusalem 'the eternal', the historical city, covers an area of only 1 sq kilometre (less than half a sq mile). Since the reign of Sultan Suleiman, nicknamed 'The Magnificent', during the middle of the 16th century, it has been surrounded by a massive wall which still stands to this day. Seven city gates, of which only three have retained their Turkish architectural style, lead into the Old City. Residents can enter by car, but visitors must approach on foot.

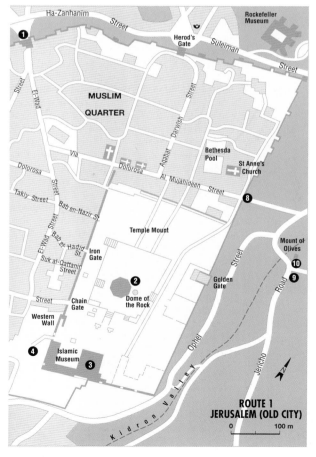

ROUTE 1
JERUSALEM (OLD CITY)

0   100 m

Over the course of history four quarters have grown up within the Old City. They are named after the religious affiliation of their inhabitants, who for centuries have lived in the area surrounding their individual religious centres. The Muslim Quarter includes the Temple Mount with its two large mosques and the bazaar street (access via the Damascus Gate or Herod's Gate). Only Jews are permitted to live in the Jewish Quarter to the west of the Western Wall (access via the Zion or Dung Gate). In the Christian Quarter lie the Church of the Holy Sepulchre and several dozen monasteries and churches (access via the Jaffa Gate or the New Gate). Finally, the Armenian Quarter surrounding the Cathedral of St James is the quietest within the Old City (access via the Jaffa Gate).

Damascus Gate

The Muslim Quarter, with its teeming bazaar, one of the most impressive in the Middle East, is entered through the massive ★★ **Damascus Gate** ❶, built in 1537. El Wad Street runs along the boundary between the Muslim and the Christian Quarters, finally intersecting with the Via Dolorosa (Al Mujahedeen Street) (*see page 27*). The latter provides access to the ★★★ **Temple Mount** (Haram esch-Scharif), dominated by the various Muslim shrines.

Dome of the Rock

The golden dome of the ★★★ **Dome of the Rock** ❷ is the city's most famous landmark. The octagonal mosque, built in 691 by Caliph Malik on the Temple Mount, is one of the three most sacred monuments of Islam. According to tradition it was from the rock (Mount Moriah) above which the dome was constructed that the Prophet Mohammed rode into heaven on his mare El Buraq ('Lightning'). Tour guides are pleased to have the chance of showing visitors the hoof marks left by the horse on the rock. The exterior walls of the 36-metre (115-ft) high mosque are clad in marble and turquoise or blue tiles. Round the top edge of the octagon runs the text of the first *surah* (chapter) of the Koran, a masterpiece of calligraphy. Of the four entrance portals, the one leading in the direction of Mecca (south) is the loveliest. The west portal is the only one providing access to the mosque.

The dome's interior is borne by two rows of pillars. Their different styles and the Greek and Byzantine capitals betray the fact that they originated in other churches. Beside the great rock stands a magnificent reliquary containing a hair from the beard of the Prophet. Legend says the souls of the departed gather in the cave known as the *Bir el Arwah*, the 'Fountain of Souls' beneath the rock.

Only a stone's throw from the Dome of the Rock, Caliph Abdul Walid, the son of Malik, built the largest mosque in the city in 714, the ★★ **El Aqsa Mosque** ❸. The seven aisles which characterise its final form were the work of Caliph Az-Zahir in 1033. Magnificent pillars support the

Detail, Dome of the Rock

Dome of the Rock

arches between the aisles. Of particular note is the interior of the Prayer Niche (*mirhab*), a gift of Sultan Saladin.

On the Temple Square also stands the ★★ **Dome of the Chain**, visually akin to the Dome of the Rock, though smaller. One legend says it derives from King David's practice of attaching heretics to a chain so that they would be struck by lightning. An alternative version is that an accused was considered innocent if he could hold the chain but guilty if the chain disappeared when grasped.

There is no charge for visiting the Temple Mount; entrance tickets for the two mosques and the Islamic Museum on the Temple Mount can be obtained from a kiosk between the El Aqsa Mosque and the Islamic Museum (Saturday to Thursday 7.30am–10am and 12.30pm–3pm).

Situated to the west of Temple Mount, the **Jewish Quarter** was inhabited by Jews as far back as the First Temple Period 3,000 years ago. Today it is a modern neighbourhood housing nearly 700 families, with numerous synagogues and *yeshivas* (academies for Jewish studies). This thriving little community was literally rebuilt out of the rubble following the the reunification of Jerusalem in the 1967 Six-Day War. Religious Jews revived many of the old study houses and congregations. Artists, attracted by the picturesque lanes, soon took up residence.

The ★★★ **Western Wall** ❹ (signposted in Hebrew as Hakotel ha Maarav and often known as the Wailing Wall) is the most sacred site for followers of the Jewish faith. It borders the southwest side of the Temple Mount. The best time to experience at first hand the profound religious significance of the Wall for devout Jews is on Friday evening. After sunset, elegantly dressed young men approach from the Jewish Quarter in groups to greet the Sabbath in song on the square in front of the Western Wall. Black-clad *Hassidim* from Mea She'arim, which lies

23

Hassids in the Jewish Quarter

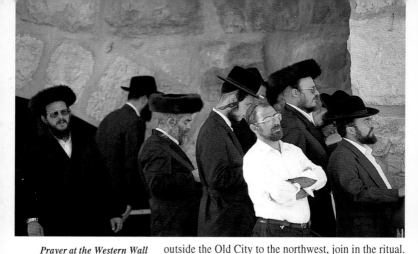

Prayer at the Western Wall

God's Letter-Box

outside the Old City to the northwest, join in the ritual.

The Western Wall forms part of the supporting wall surrounding the Temple Mount. It was constructed by Herod during his enlargement of the hill. This section of the wall acquired its nickname because it was here that the Jews wailed when lamenting the destruction of their temple by the Roman emperor Titus in 70AD. Later, after the Bar-Kochba Uprising (135AD), they were forbidden even to approach the area.

The site of the First and Second temples is immediately above the 18-m (58-ft) high wall on the plateau of the Temple Mount. The original length of the West Wall was about 500 metres. Until 1967 only about one-tenth was accessible, primarily because over the centuries the houses of the Old Town had been built in places as close as 4m (13ft) to the wall, thus permitting only restricted access via a narrow alley in front of the wall itself. After the conquest of East Jerusalem the Israelis demolished these houses and laid out a wide open square. The section of the wall accessible to the pious was extended by means of excavations to its present length of approximately 170 metres.

On closer examination, the visitor will notice that great numbers of small scraps of paper with writing on them have been pushed into the gaps in between the vast limestone blocks. They contain wishes, requests or thanks from pious Jews directly to the Lord. For this reason the Western Wall is also known as 'God's Letter-Box'. These should not be read by anyone except God; however, the 'postbox' also requires emptying from time to time when it becomes over-full. Thus once a month the Supreme Rabbinical Council has the notes removed at night from the cracks and buried anonymously on the Mount of Olives.

Every day, from early morning until late at night, prayers are said by the Western Wall. Many devout Jews emphasise their prayers by violent movements. Men and women pray separately. Men are required to cover their heads as they approach the wall; women must cover their shoulders and legs. Photography is permitted except on the Sabbath.

From the large square in front of the Western Wall, the tour can continue through the Jewish Quarter along Tiferet Street with the remarkable ★ **Burnt House**, an archaeological site which was once the residence of the priestly Bar Kathros clan at the time of the Jewish revolt against the Rome. Ashes indicate that the house was destroyed when Titus razed the city. The numerous finds within the house include in the kitchen the skeletal arm of a woman who apparently was struggling to escape the fire.

The Jewish Quarter

The **Jewish Quarter Museum** in Jewish Quarter Street offers a 15-minute multimedia presentation on the history of the area from the Israelite period to the present. The most enchanting of the Quarter's venerable houses of worship are on Hakehuna Street in the complex known as the ★★ **Four Sephardi Synagogues**, which have been lovingly restored to serve as both houses of worship and as a museum documenting their destruction and rebirth.

25

The most direct way of reaching the **Christian Quarter** from the Western Wall, it is to follow Bab es-Silsila Street and Souk el-Attarin. The ★★ **Church of the Redeemer** ❺ was dedicated in 1898 in the presence of the German emperor Wilhelm II. It stands on the foundations of an earlier church built in about 1000AD whose cloister still stands today. The church tower affords a remarkable view across the Old City (9am–1pm and 2pm–5pm, Friday 9am–1pm).

Church of the Holy Sepulchre

In the immediate vicinity will also be found the principal Christian shrine in Jerusalem, the ★★★ **Church of the Holy Sepulchre** ❻. Every morning, Wajeeh Nuseibeh, a friendly Palestinian Muslim, opens the heavy wooden doors of the church and closes them again at night. He is at present the eldest son of the local family to which Sultan Saladin entrusted the keys to Christianity's most sacred site during the 12th century. He did so because the various confessions fought especially at night over the best places in the church. In order to bring this unfriendly rivalry to a peaceful conclusion, the priests of all confessions living in the Church of the Holy Sepulchre were locked into their quarters every night – and this ritual is still performed today by Wajeeh Nuseibeh.

The Church of the Holy Sepulchre was built between 326 and 335 by the Emperor Constantine at his mother's insistence. It stands above the site where the crucifixion, burial and resurrection of Jesus are believed to have taken place. It was destroyed several times – in 614 by the Persians, in 1009 by the Shiite Fatimid Caliph Hakim, and

Priest at the church of the Holy Sepulchre

again by fire in 1808 – but is was always rebuilt. The most elaborate reconstruction was the one in 1149 under the Crusaders, but it lost its original form of a basilica. Furthermore, the centuries-old struggle between the Eastern and Western church for a share in the building also resulted in the architectural muddle of chapels, pictures, pillars, statues and ceiling frescoes which sometimes confuses the modern visitor.

Today, this labyrinth of religiosity houses six Christian confessions: the Catholics, the Armenians, the Greek Orthodox, the Syrian Orthodox, the Coptics and the Ethiopians. The latter have owned since the 4th century a small monastery on the roof of the church (Deir es- Sultan). Each confession has its own niches and chapels; it seems as if every square metre has been divided up according to the status quo of the year 1852, an agreement into which they were forced by the Turkish sultan of the time. Even the State of Israel does not interfere.

All confessions share the over-decorated **Chapel of the Holy Sepulchre**. In the middle is a small marble-tiled room with a two-metre gravestone covering Jesus's tomb. Only a handful of people can enter the room at a time, so access is controlled by a male member of each of the confessions. The six guards are replaced regularly according to a strictly observed plan. At each change large quantities of incense are used to help to cover the traces of the predecessor. The changes take place so punctually that you can set your watch by them, for no devout Christian will file past the tomb of the Saviour without humbly slipping a coin into the outstretched hand of the watchman. Visitors in search of pious tranquillity are in the wrong place here.

David's Tower

The tour arrives at the ★★ **Jaffa Gate** beside the ★★ **Citadel** or **David's Tower** ❼. Here once stood the palace of Herod the Great, whose landmark consisted of three forbidding towers built of huge stone blocks. Destroyed by the Romans and built over several times since, today the citadel has assumed once more very much the form it received during the 16th century under Suleiman the Magnificent. A visit to the **Museum of Municipal History** within the citadel is very worthwhile (Sunday to Thursday 10am–5pm, Friday 10am–2pm).

Armenian Patriarchate Street leads around the Citadel up from the David Street bazaar, passing through a brief tunnel before entering the **Armenian Quarter**. A modest doorway leads to the Armenians' **St James Cathedral** ❽, one of the most impressive churches in the Old City. The **Armenian Museum**, a graceful cloister housing a fascinating collection of manuscripts and artefacts, is a little further on. Jerusalem's 2,000 or so Armenians live in

a tightly knit community behind the Cathedral-museum complex. Armenian Patriarchate Road leads out through Zion Gate to Mount Zion, where the **Cenacle**, believed to be the Room of the Last Supper, and the Benedictine **Dormition Abbey** commemorating the place where Mary fell into eternal sleep, are the principal attractions.

The ★★★ **Via Dolorosa** begins at the **St Stephen's Gate** ❾. It leads via nine Stations of the Cross through the Old City to the Church of the Holy Sepulchre (*see page 25*). Every Friday afternoon a procession of Franciscan monks follows Christ's route of suffering. Their starting point is the courtyard of the Medersa El-Omariya, a Muslim boys' institution; King Herod's Antonia Fortress, where Jesus was sentenced to death, once stood in the vicinity. Today, the Via Dolorosa is a commercial street, complete with a Jesus Prison Souvenirs shop and a Ninth Station Boutique. The last five stations are found in the Church of the Holy Sepulchre.

Mount of Olives

The ★★★ **Mount of Olives**, from where Jesus is said to have made his triumphal entry into Jerusalem, is some 100m (320ft) higher than the Old City. The walk across the **Mount** begins in the ★ **Garden of Gethsemane** ❿. The gnarled olive trees in the garden are said to date from Biblical times: it is claimed that they stood here when Christ prayed in the garden before being betrayed by Judas and arrested. It has been suggested that Judas hanged himself from one of these trees.

Adjacent to the garden is the Catholic ★ **Church of All Nations**, noted for its fine Byzantine-style mosaic facade; its 12 cupolas represent the 12 nations that contributed towards its construction, which was completed in 1924.

Via Dolorosa

27

Ancient olive trees,
Garden of Gethsemane
Church of All Nations

Bell-tower, Tomb of the Virgin

Security at the Mount of Olives

Nearby is the ★★ **Tomb of the Virgin** ⓫, lying deep within the earth and lit by candles of Orthodox Christian churches. Midway down the stairs to the 5th-century chapel are niches said to hold the remains of Mary's parents, Joachim and Anne, and her husband Joseph.

Halfway up the mountain is the Russian Orthodox-**Church of Mary Magdalene**, easily identifiable by its golden onion-domes. It was built by Czar Alexander III in 1873. The summit is dominated by the Russian Orthodox **Church of the Ascension** with its landmark belltower. On the far side of the mount, with view of the Judean Desert and the red hills of Edom across the Jordan, is the **Bethpage Chapel**, from where the Palm Sunday processions to Jerusalem begin.

The view of the Holy City from the summit will make even non-Jews understand the symbolic word of farewell 'Next Year in Jerusalem!' with which Jews often take their leave of each other, even if they do not live in the city.

Modern Jerusalem

The sites of modern Jerusalem are grouped around **Mount Herzl** ⓬, the site of the sarcophagus of the spiritual father of Zionism. Here also stands the Israeli ★ **Knesset** ⓭. A highlight of any visit to Jerusalem, and one which should not be missed on any account, is the ★★ **Israel Museum** ⓮ (Sunday to Thursday 10am–6pm, Tuesday 10am–10pm; *bus: 9, 17, 24*), which houses several collections under one roof: The **Bezalel Art Museum** contains French Impressionist paintings; the **Samuel Bronfman Museum** is an archaeological collection displaying the results of excavations in the region, the **Billy Rose Garden** is a sculpture garden with works by Auguste Rodin and Henry Moore and the white domed building visible from afar is the ★ **Shrine of the Book**, housing the most valuable religious writings documenting the religious history of Judaism, the 1st-century Qumran Scrolls (*see page 73*) which were found beside the Dead Sea.

Shrine of the Book

The shape of the roof, which is covered with gleaming white tiles, echoes that of the lid of the amphora in which the scrolls on exhibition were discovered. The dark underground approach is also designed to convey an impression of the cave in Qumran where the scrolls were found. The black wall on the side of the white domed building reflects the words of one of the Essenian texts: 'The struggle between the powers of darkness and light'.

Such is the value of the scrolls that most of the exhibits on display are replicas. In the middle of the dome, arranged like a Torah scroll, are the famous Isaiah texts.

Opposite are two newer attractions, the **Bible Lands Museum** and the **Bloomfield Museum of Science**.

Yad Vashem

The national monument ★★ **Yad Vashem** on Mount Hazz-
ikaron in the west of Jerusalem (Sunday to Thursday
9am–5pm, Friday 9am–4pm) recalls the extermination
(Hebrew: Shoa) of 6 million European Jews under the Nazi
regime. It is the most important memorial in Israel. The
Hall of Remembrance, in the floor of which are engraved
the names of the main concentration and extermination
camps, lies in solemn semi-darkness.

Grief at Yad Vashem

The monument also includes a documentation and
research centre and an art gallery exhibiting works by
Holocaust survivors. Particularly striking is the exhibition
'Warning and Witness', in which the history of the Jewish
race in Europe during the years from 1938 to 1945 is doc-
umented. After visiting Yad Vashem and being reminded
of the grim fate of the Jews during the Nazi era, the traveller will look with more understanding on many aspects

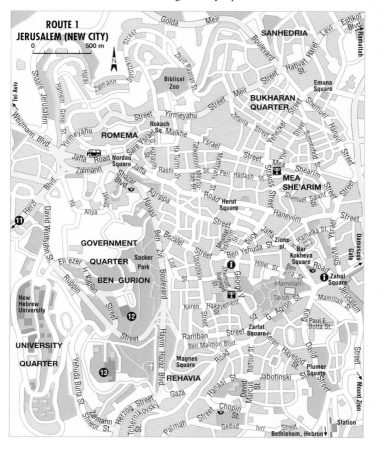

ROUTE 1
JERUSALEM (NEW CITY)
0   500 m

of modern Israel and its people's priorities. Visitors approach the memorial along gravel paths which lead through the Garden of the Righteous. On either side of the path, also known as the Avenue of the Righteous, are trees with small nameplates honouring those non-Jews declared to be the 'Righteous amongst the Peoples'. These individuals, including such famous names as Oskar Schindler, demonstrated great courage by supporting persecuted Jews during the Holocaust, thus gaining the highest decoration Israel offers to non-Jews.

Excursions

Bethlehem

Bethlehem today

According to Biblical sources, ★★★ **Bethlehem** was the birthplace of King David and, 1,000 years later, of Jesus. The little town lies only 12km (7½ miles) south of Jerusalem in the Palestinian territory of West Jordan (the West Bank). The first visitors to Bethlehem (Hebrew: 'The House of Bread') on the occasion of Christ's birth were shepherds from the surrounding fields, who came on foot. They were followed by the Three Kings who, on account of the gifts they bore and the increased distance, travelled on horseback and by camel. Nowadays tourists take a Sherut taxi by the Damascus Gate and can reach the Church of the Nativity in 15 minutes. Bethlehem has 38,000 inhabitants, of whom the majority are Muslim and fewer than 10,000 Christian.

In Roman times Bethlehem enjoyed great strategic significance because it provided control over the road to Masada. It was not until the reign of the Emperor Constantine that the town acquired its symbolic importance as the birthplace of Jesus. When Christianity became the state

Church of the Nativity

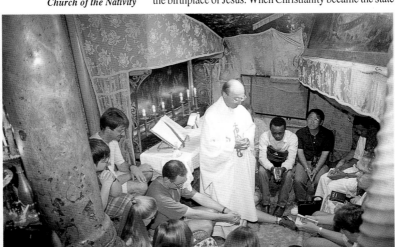

religion of the Roman Empire in 326, St Helena, mother of the first Christian Roman emperor (Constantine I), had a basilica constructed over the Grotto of the Nativity at the suggestion of the Bishop of Jerusalem. It was dedicated with great ceremony in 339. Together with the Mount of Olives (Mount of the Ascension) and the Holy Sepulchre (Resurrection), both in Jerusalem, Bethlehem immediately became one of the three most important early Christian sites in Palestine.

Church of the Nativity

The ★★★ **Church of the Nativity** (daily 8am–6pm) lies at the heart of the city on Manger Square. It acquired its present countenance in 529 under the Emperor Justinian, who had the basilica rebuilt because it had suffered heavy damage during an uprising. Since then the church's physical appearance has changed little. It was here that, 500 years later, on Christmas Eve 1100, the Crusaders crowned Baldwin I as the first ruler of the Kingdom of Jerusalem. The coronation took place in Bethlehem because Baldwin did not want to be crowned King of Jerusalem with 'a crown of gold and precious stones' in the Church of the Holy Sepulchre, where 'Our Lord once wore the Crown of Thorns'.

31

Little light penetrates the rectangular nave with five aisles and four lofty rows of columns. In the apse-like niche of the **Grotto of the Nativity**, which lies at a lower level and which is about 12m (38ft) long, there is a 14-pointed silver star on the floor. It was placed there in 1717 by the Catholic Church and since then has been held to mark the exact birthplace of the Saviour. The Latin inscription on the star recalls the event: '*Hic de virgine Maria Jesus Christus natus est*' ('Here Jesus Christ was born of the Virgin Mary'). Next to the ornate grotto is the **Chapel of the Manger**, where Mary placed the newborn.

In the Church of the Nativity, the strife amongst the various Christian confessions is similar to that governing the Church of the Holy Sepulchre. The problem has been especially acute since 1855, when the Turkish sultan placed the church under the jurisdiction of the Greek Orthodox community. Now only three major Christian confessions have a part-share in the Church of the Nativity, but each of them celebrates the birth of Jesus on a different day. The Catholics (and with them the Melkites, the Maronites and the Syrian Catholic Church) celebrate the feast of Christmas on 24 December. For the Greek and Syrian Orthodox Eastern churches (and with them the Coptic and Ethiopian Christians) Christmas falls on 6 January. Finally, the Armenians don't hold their Christmas celebrations until 18 January.

Getting oriented in Bethlehem

The confessions are also divided as to the location of the field where the shepherds heard the glad tidings: sign-

St Catherine's Church and Milk Grotto Church

posts outside the town offer a choice between a Catholic, a Greek Orthodox and a Protestant hillside. Clustered around the Church of the Nativity are several churches of varying Christian denominations. The most famous on Christmas Eve is **St Catherine's Church**, from which Bethlehem's annual Midnight Mass is broadcast worldwide. Those without a ticket can watch the Mass on a huge screen in Manger Square, or see the service being broadcast live on Israel's main television channel.

The ★ **Milk Grotto Church** is a short walk down Milk Grotto Street. Legend has it that, while nursing the newborn Jesus, some of Mary's milk splashed to the stone floor and permanently whitened it. Today stone scrapings are sold to pilgrims to enable better breastfeeding.

Mar Saba

From Bethlehem it is only 15km (9 miles) to the famous blue domes of the Greek Orthodox monastery of **Mar Saba** (Monday to Saturday 9am–noon), built on a rocky hillside. It lies on the south bank of the River Kidron, which has gouged a deep channel through the limestone plateau. The monastery complex is a closely packed collection of interlinked houses above the steeply sloping river bed. It was founded in 492 by St Saba. To this day its charnel house continues to hold the skulls of all the monks who have lived in Mar Saba, including those who defended the monastery in 614. The complex is inhabited nowadays by only a dozen monks of Greek and Russian origins. The Main Church boasts an important icon altar. One of the twin watchtowers is known as the 'Women's Tower' because from here women, who are not allowed to enter the monastery, can get a glimpse of the interior.

Hebron

Glass blower, Hebron

The Arab town of ★ **Hebron** (Arabic: El Khalil) lies in the heart of the hills of Judea, 26km (16 miles) south of Bethlehem. Hebron is the site of the tombs of the three patriarchs Abraham, Isaac and Jacob and their wives, and it was here that David was anointed king before he moved his seat of government to Jerusalem.

The most important site in Hebron is ★ **Haram el Khalil**. Herod the Great was the first ruler to fortify the burial place of the patriarchs by constructing massive walls around the Machpelah Cave. Emperor Justinian had a church built here; this was later turned into a mosque and then converted back into a basilica by the Crusaders. The Mamelukes who succeeded them gave the building its present-day appearance as the Ibrahim Mosque, although only two of the four minarets added by them remain.

Route 2

By the beach in Tel Aviv

★ Tel Aviv – the metropolis by the sea

During the warmer months, many 'Tel-Avivniks', as the city's inhabitants are known throughout Israel, begin their day on the beach. The beach is at its pleasantest in the morning and evening, when the shadows are long and the water is still an agreeable 26˚C (79˚F). The promenade is lined with hundreds of white deck chairs, encouraging visitors to linger. Immediately behind the beach stand the high-rises of the international hotel chains, dominating the skyline.

33

Tel Aviv is Israel's principal commercial and industrial city. It is also an expanding business centre and the country's cultural arena – in short, Israel's secret capital. Its 350,000 inhabitants make it the largest city in the country after Jerusalem. However, if one includes the new dormitory suburbs which have grown up on the edge of the city to the north, east and south – Ramat Gan, Giva Tayim and Bat Yam – the Tel Aviv metropolitan area has a population of well over 1 million.

IBM building and Bank Haopolim

It is said that Jerusalem is sacred, and Tel Aviv secular: several theatres, a large number of cinemas, the only philharmonic orchestra in the Middle East, pop concerts and a yacht marina certainly offer a wide range of worldly pleasures. When Iraqi rockets hit the Cultural Centre in the spring of 1991, the Mayor, Shlomo Lahat, had it rebuilt immediately – larger and more beautiful than ever. It is claimed that he told the municipal treasurer, who was groaning at the city's financial debts, that music, theatre, ballet and film were essential to life itself. In the evening, Jerusalem residents like to drive over to worldly Tel Aviv – this is particularly popular on the Sabbath, not least because of the beach.

Unlike elsewhere in Israel, the past is not tangible in Tel Aviv, and only those who seek it will find it in the city's museums or in Jaffa.

History

A historic photograph dating from 1908 at the entrance of the Independence Museum portrays 50 well-dressed men who are standing looking somewhat out of place amongst the sand dunes along the beach north of Jaffa. They have formed a circle, in the middle of which stands a man who is making a speech. Apart from that, the picture shows nothing but sand. The photo depicts the moment when Tel Aviv was born, a city founded by Jews who had emigrated from Europe to Palestine in the spirit of the new Zionist philosophy and marked by the ideals of a humanistic and socially just society. They had all read Theodor Herzl's visionary book *The Jewish State*, and were laying the foundation stone for the first solely Jewish town in Palestine. The photograph shows Meir Dizengoff, who was later to become mayor, drawing lots for the first 60 parcels of land on the 'Hill of Spring' – the meaning of the Hebrew name Tel Aviv.

During the 1930s, Tel Aviv became a refuge for European immigrants and, by 1948, its population of 150,000 made it the largest town in Palestine. After 14 May 1948, when David Ben-Gurion proclaimed the independence of Israel in what was then the municipal museum, Tel Aviv was even the capital of the new country until December 1949 when the government moved to Jerusalem.

On 13 May 1948 the Arab town of Jaffa surrendered to the Jewish army. Almost the entire population abandoned the town and set off in the direction of Gaza, leaving behind only 500 Palestinian families. In 1950 Jaffa was incorporated into the urban area of Tel Aviv. Since then, the city's official name has been Tel Aviv-Yafo.

Since 1974, the town has been governed by Shlomo Lahat, who was born in 1927 in Berlin and whose name was Salo Lindner until his parents emigrated to Palestine in 1933. He is a popular Likud Party politician who has turned the city into a world metropolis.

Sights

The starting point for a tour of Tel Aviv is ★ **Dizengoff Circle** (Kikar Zina) ❶, a raised piazza named after the first mayor's wife, Zina. Skilful traffic management in the middle of Dizengoff Boulevard, the city's best-known grand avenue, has created a square which has become one of the main focal points of city life. In the centre stands a fountain by the Israeli artist Yaacov Agam, who has combined the contrasting elements of fire and water into an interplay between rotating jets of water and burning gas

34

Around Dizengoff Circle

Dizengoff Centre

flames. Every hour on the hour the spectacle begins to the accompaniment of music.

Continue along Dizengoff Boulevard to arrive at the **★★ Cultural Centre ❷** and the neighbouring **Helena Rubinstein Museum**, which displays an interesting collection of works by contemporary Israeli artists (Sunday to Wednesday 10am–5pm, Thursday 10am–10pm, Saturday 10am–3pm). Performances by the Israel Philharmonic Orchestra take place in the **Frederic Mann Auditorium**. Not far away stands the **Habimah Theatre ❸**. This fine example of Bauhaus architecture in Israel was built in 1935 on the square of the same name in accordance with the plans drawn up by the Berlin architect Oskar Kaufmann.

Checking out the route

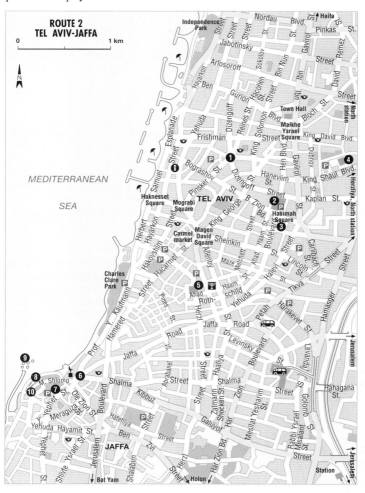

ROUTE 2 TEL AVIV–JAFFA

0   1 km

MEDITERRANEAN SEA

TEL AVIV

JAFFA

It is one of some 4,000 Bauhaus buildings – many of them under protection order – which characterise Tel Aviv's contemporary countenance. Their architects, notably Arieh Sharon, Shmuel Miestechkin, Munio Weinraub and Zeev Rechter, had studied in Germany under Walter Gropius and Ludwig Mies van der Rohe before emigrating to Palestine after the Bauhaus was closed by the Nazis in 1933. Their ideas, also influenced by Le Corbusier and Erich Mendelssohn, found expression in the rapidly expanding city, where the typical flat roofs and smooth white facades with vertical windows and surrounding balconies proved ideal for the climatic conditions.

Shalom Tower

The modern **Tel Aviv Museum ❹** (Sunday to Wednesday 10am–5pm, Thursday 12 noon–10pm, Saturday 10am–3pm) also displays works by present-day Israeli artists. The building itself enjoys world fame as a role model for museum buildings. The older wing of the museum on Rothschild Boulevard (Independence Hall) is a historic site, for it was here that the independence of Israel was declared in 1948.

★ **Migdal Shalom ❺** on Ahad Haam Street (daily except Saturday 9am–5pm, Friday until 2pm), is the tallest building in Tel Aviv. With its height of 140m (448ft) it dwarfs the southern part of the city. The skyscraper stands on the site of the Herzliyya, a famous grammar school, which Shalom Mayer, a millionaire, reputedly demolished in an act of vengeance; he was once a pupil there. Within the building are a shopping centre, restaurants, offices and even a **Waxworks Museum**. The most interesting aspect is the **Observation Platform** on the 34th floor which offers one of the most impressive views of the city.

On the Ramat Aviv university campus north of the Yarkon River is the interesting ★★ **Beit Ha-Tefuzot** museum, which relates the 2,000-year history of the Jews in the Diaspora by means of an excellent multimedia show (Sunday to Thursday 10am–5pm, Wednesday until 7pm).

The **Etzel** museum in Kaufmann Street describes the Israeli-Arab conflict in the Tel Aviv-Yafo region and during the War of Independence from the Zionist perspective (Sunday to Thursday 8.30am–3pm, Friday and Saturday 8.30am–12 noon).

Jaffa

Outdoor market, Jaffa

If we are to believe the Biblical account, the Arab town of Jaffa was built by Japhet, Noah's youngest son, after the Flood. Archaeological discoveries reveal that the port has existed since 2000BC. It was via Jaffa that the cedars of Lebanon used by Solomon for the construction of the First Temple were shipped to Jerusalem. The flight of the prophet Jonah began in Jaffa, and, according to Greek legend, it was in Jaffa that Andromeda was chained to a

Jaffa's old port

rock. In later times the Romans conquered the town, followed by the Crusaders under Richard the Lionheart, then by the Turkish sultans and finally by Napoleon. In 1917 the town surrendered to the British army under General Allenby. Jaffa was always the port for Jerusalem, and during the British mandate it was the port of disembarkation for many Jewish immigrants.

37

Today Jaffa is a district of Tel Aviv and a popular tourist attraction. Art galleries, jewellers' shops and antique shops line the narrow alleys. Restaurants and cafés with magnificent views of the glittering night skyline of Tel Aviv enhance the atmosphere.

Tel Aviv as seen from Jaffa

Only a stone's throw from the **Main Square** ❻ is the **Mahmudiye Mosque**, built in 1810. Its inner courtyard is adorned with the stumps of pillars from Ashkelon. Walking up the Mifratz Shlomo Promenade the visitor will pass on the left-hand side the ★ **Archaeological Museum** ❼ exhibiting interesting finds from the town's past before arriving at the ★ **Franciscan Church of St Peter** ❽, built during the 17th century on the foundations of the former fortress of Jaffa. Remains of the citadel can be inspected in the monastery cellar. The interior of the church is worth a visit for its elaborate carvings.

The monastery itself affords a fine view of the legendary **Andromeda Rock** ❾ and the old **port**. Today only fishing boats chug past the quays.

Statues near galleries, Jaffa

A staircase leads to the lively focal point of historic Jaffa, the **Kikar Kedumim** ❿. Cafés, boutiques and restaurants fringe the square, which also offers an interesting archaeological perspective. Excavations have revealed the different levels of settlement which occurred during the past, affording a cross-section through the town's 4,000 years of history. This square has become one of Tel Aviv's most popular evening spots.

Sun worshipper, Eilat

An ideal sea for windsurfing

Route 3

★ **Eilat – sun and deep blue sea**

'Every day is Sun Day' – Israel's largest seaside resort advertises its charms with this catch phrase. Its location on the southern tip of the Negev Desert, directly on the Red Sea, provides the justification. Even in mid-winter the average water temperature is 20˚C (68˚F); from July until October it is even 25˚C (77˚F). It rains perhaps a dozen times each year. During July and August the daytime temperatures often reach the 40˚C (104˚F) mark; however, low humidity makes the heat tolerable. In January, the 'coldest' month in Eilat, the thermometer doesn't sink below 21˚C (70˚F). In other words, a perfect climate, with sunshine and a deep blue sea inviting visitors to sporting activity above and below the water.

Providing a contrast to the sun-and-sea routine are desert adventures and nature encounters: safaris in the Negev, excursions to the Hai Bar Game Park, day trips to St Catherine's, one of the oldest monasteries, or to Mount Sinai on the Sinai Peninsula.

Eilat's nightlife also compares favourably with that of any major holiday resort: entertainment shows, open-air concerts, music and dancing into the small hours in nightclubs and discos. Those who prefer a quiet evening can enjoy an evening stroll along the well-kept beach promenade. When the sun sinks behind the mountains in the desert and the sea turns a fascinating purple colour, the riddle as to how the Red Sea got its name is solved.

History

Together with Aqaba, 3km (2 miles) away on the Jordanian side, Eilat can look back over a long history. The Bible reports that the Children of Israel paused on this stretch of coast during their journey through the wilderness. Later, King David conquered the region from the Edomites. Solomon built up his fleet on this spot, and it was here that he met the Queen of Sheba. In the nearby Timna Valley he had copper mined for the legendary Ophir. The Nabataeans called the port Aila; the Arabs christened it Aqaba, and the Crusaders built a fortress on the 'Pharaoh's Island', the Isle de Graye (Ha-Almuggim, 'Coral Island').

After Sultan Saladin conquered the town in 1167 the coast fell into oblivion. It was not until 800 years later, during World War I, that the name Aqaba hit the international headlines once more when Lawrence of Arabia, in alliance with the Hashemite Emir Feisal, wrested the town from the Turks.

Eilat was awarded its municipal charter in 1959, although in those days less than one-tenth of its present pop-

North beach, Eilat

ulation of 40,000 lived in the makeshift assortment of housing surrounding the little harbour. The fact that this tip of land on the Gulf of Aqaba belongs to Israel in the first place is a result of 'Operation Uvda', a manoeuvre which was contrary to the Law of Nations. On 13 March 1949, following the armistice agreement at the end of the War of Independence, two Israeli brigades simply occupied a coastal strip several miles long opposite the town of Aqaba, between Jordan and Egypt. During the following years the Israelis enlarged the quays along the harbour front, constructed an oil terminal and improved the road connection through the Negev to Beersheba. The road through the Arava Valley to the Dead Sea was not completed until 1967.

The peace agreement between Israel and the Palestinians and the Kingdom of Jordan has led to ambitious frontier-free expansion schemes at the Gulf of Aqaba. The planners dream of transforming the entire coastal strip from the Saudi Arabian border (20km/13 miles south of Aqaba) to a point well down the Sinai Peninsula into the largest holiday paradise in the entire Middle East which will completely ignore national boundaries. The planners hope that, by the end of the century, Eilat alone will have doubled its hotel capacity to 10,000 beds.

Sights

Visitors will search in vain in present-day Eilat – as well as in Aqaba across the border in Jordan – for sights recalling the town's 3,000-year history. The only traces of past times will be found in the Timna Valley and on the Isle de Graye south of Taba (*see pages 41 and 42*). Eilat, however, can boast a number of modern attractions which should not be missed.

★ **Coral World** (Underwater Observatory), a 'Museum in the Sea' (Saturday to Thursday 8.30am–4.30pm, Fri-

Underwater observatory

The view from inside the underwater observatory

Dolphins in action

40

day 8.30am–3pm) can be reached via a walkway from Coral Beach. It is like an aquarium in reverse, where the exotic fish swim outside in freedom and the human observers are 'imprisoned' under the sea. A spiral staircase enables visitors to keep their feet dry as they descend to the sea bed. Gazing through the bull's-eye windows, you can observe the fascinating coral world of the Red Sea.

Additional attractions are provided by the **submarines.** The *Jules Verne*, a modern red luxury vessel, travels as a mobile underwater observatory through the Gulf of Aqaba along the coral reefs. After dark it offers an 'Underwater Laser Show'. Departures are from the Harbour North Beach.

Jacqueline is the name of the 'Yellow Submarine' which uses the popular Beatles song to advertise its services. The one-hour underwater trip, during which you can observe the underwater world to a depth of 60m/192ft through bull's eyes, begins next door to the Coral World Underwater Observatory.

Eilat's latest attraction, **Dolphin Reef**, provides a chance to swim around and play underwater (without a diving certificate) with a school of seven adult dolphins (daily 9am–6pm). The pool is directly on the coral coast, so that the 'nature experience' – at least on the photographs – appears perfect.

Eilat offers ideal conditions for learning to dive, from a test dive to the acquisition of a diving certificate. Half a dozen diving schools offer their services year-round. One of the largest is the **Red Sea Sports Club**, which has two diving centres in Eilat and advertises the fact that its team of instructors includes 'high-ranking teachers from the Israeli army'. Diving mostly takes place off Coral Beach in the south of Eilat. This is a protected coral reef a few yards from the shore.

The first weightless experience of the brightly coloured coral world after many hours of practice in the swimming pool, the sight of thousands of multi-coloured fish swimming past at a depth of 10m (30ft), the perfect silence which is only interrupted by the sound of the air bubbles rising to the surface and the breathing sounds of the breathing equipment will make the visitor a lifelong fan of this fascinating sport.

Experienced divers value Eilat as a starting point for diving excursions along the east Sinai coast. The region is considered to be one of the finest diving grounds in the world, especially the areas by the southern tip near Sharm el-Sheikh and Ras Muhammed.

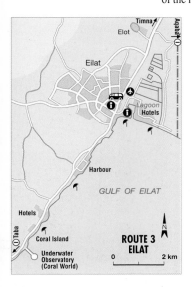

ROUTE 3 EILAT

0   2 km

Timna

Elot

Aqaba

Eilat

Lagoon Hotels

Harbour

GULF OF EILAT

Hotels

Taba

Coral Island

Underwater Observatory (Coral World)

N

Isle de Graye/Pharaoh's Island

Some 15km/ 9 miles south of Eilat, approximately 250m
from the shore on Egyptian territory, lies the Isle de Graye,
the 'Coral Island' (Ha-Almuggum/Djeziret Fara'un). As
a result of its Arab name it is popularly known as the
'Pharaoh's Island'. Measuring just 300m long by 150m
wide, the island was chosen in 1116 by the Crusaders as
the site for a fortress from which they could control the
routes between Egypt and the Arabian Peninsula. The
Knights of the Cross also used it as a base from which they
set out on raids into Arab territory.

The ruins occupy the northern half of the island. Large
sections of the west wall, massive arches, the towers and
the keep can still be seen. A mosque with prayer niche
(*mihrab*) in the southern part indicates that the buildings
were later used by the Mamelukes and Turks.

Mount Sinai and ★★ St Catherine's Monastery

A one- or two-day trip into the Sinai Peninsula offers a
magnificent drive through imposing desert landscapes and,
on Mount Sinai (Gebel Mûsa), a glimpse of the beginnings
of Biblical history. The necessary Egyptian visa can be obtained at the frontier. If you book an organised tour through
one of the Israeli tour operators in Eilat, the visa charges
are somewhat lower.

41

It was on the summit of the **Mount Sinai** (2,285m/
7,312ft), which can be reached after a climb of several
hours, that Moses received the Ten Commandments. Today a small chapel stands on the site. Although the chapel
is permanently closed, it is the goal of many pilgrims who
walk up during the evening or at night from St Catherine's
Monastery in order to witness the sunrise on the far side
of the Red Sea behind the peaks of the Sinai Mountains.

High on Mount Sinai

St Catherine's Monastery

It is a sight which belongs to one of the great natural experiences on the Sinai Peninsula.

At the foot of the mountain, where God manifested Himself to Moses in the miracle of the Burning Bush, the Emperor's mother Helena erected in about 330 a church for Christian hermits. Becoming a monastery during the 12th century, it was given the name of St Catherine because the saint's bones were found here. ★★ **St Catherine's Monastery** is one of the oldest in the world; its stock of books and icons goes back to the 5th century. Also of interest is the charnel house, in which the skulls of the monks who died in the monastery were preserved. Visitors may spend the night in the monastery's guest house.

Timna Valley

Mushroom Rock, Timna National Park

The **Timna Valley**, whose steep gorges have been declared a National Park, lies 25km (16 miles) north of Eilat. The park covers and area of 50sq km (19 sq miles) and can only be visited in a rented car or by coach as the principal sites lie some distance from each other.

They include the **Pillars of Solomon**, 50-m (160-ft) high sandstone columns carved by the wind out of the rock walls. Erosion has created the **Mushroom Rock**, an oversized free-standing block of worn sandstone popular with photographers. Also of interest are the **Timna Copper Mines**, in which copper was mined using open-cast methods during the reign of King Solomon. The archaeologist who excavated King Solomon's Mines called the ventilation system 'an early example of automation'.

Hai Bar

North of the Timna Valley National Park, the Kibbutz Yotvata maintains an unusual nature reserve. It is aimed to provide a home for all the animals mentioned in the Bible in the **Hai Bar Wildlife Sanctuary** (daily 8am–3pm).

Hai Bar lies in a region which has a relatively good water supply, which explains the luxuriant vegetation, the trees and willows in the otherwise gaunt, rocky limestone landscape. Driving along the visitor's route, one can observe the animals at the waterholes and feeding places. Since many animals of biblical times have long since become extinct in Israel, or no longer live here in the wild, breeding attempts are also being undertaken in Hai Bar.

There are also 10 signposted footpaths leading through the park. Large glass walls with one-way vision have been installed at the feeding places so that visitors can observe the birds and beasts of prey at close quarters without being seen, heard or smelt by the animals.

Route 4

Haifa and its bay

★★ Haifa – the town by Mount Carmel

Gazing across the breathtaking panorama of Haifa Bay from Gan Haem, the mountain station of the Carmelit Railway, the visitor will understand why Haifa is considered to be one of the most beautiful cities in the world. For thousands of years men have been drawn by the charm radiating from the natural harmony of the relationship between sea and mountain. And yet Haifa, with its 300,000 inhabitants, is also the third-largest city in Israel – and one of the few places in the Holy Land which is not mentioned in the Bible. Nonetheless, it can still claim its place in Biblical history, for it lies on the slopes of Mount Carmel.

43

Cybernetics at the bio-med faculty

History

The mountain ridge of Mount Carmel is one of the oldest regions in Palestine to be settled; in Biblical times it was clad in vineyards. Today, wines produced here have earned an international reputation. The prophet Isaiah called Carmel 'God's Vineyard' (Kerem El), and at times a cave on its slopes served Elijah as a refuge. The name of Haifa first occurs in the Talmudic Scriptures (Hof yaffe, meaning 'Beautiful Shore').

Until the 12th century, Haifa was a little village overshadowed by Acco, in which Jews and Muslims lived side by side in peace. In 1100 it was conquered by the Crusaders, who murdered the inhabitants and made the place the administrative headquarters of the Seigneurie Caiphas. After the expulsion of the Crusaders the settlement was razed to the ground. Although Haifa had been known since the 2nd century as a safe haven for passing ships, situated as it was along one of the Mediterranean's oldest sealanes, it was not until the 18th century that it experienced

Elijah's cave, Haifa

a modest prosperity under Sheikh El-Omar. The German colony of the Knights Templar, founded in 1869, contributed to the town's European air. Today the colony lies at the southern end of Ben-Gurion Street. The Zionist immigrants at the beginning of the 20th century also played their part after Theodor Herzl had praised Haifa as the 'Town of the Future'.

Also important for the economic development of Haifa was the construction of the railway line to Damascus, which linked the town to the Hedschas Railway in 1905. A few years later, in 1912, German Zionists founded the Technikon, the first Technical University in the Middle East. Later, when space became short in the inner city, it was moved to the slopes of Mount Carmel. After the port was extended at the end of the 1920s, 'British' Haifa competed with 'French' Beirut for supremacy as the prime commercial centre in the Middle East.

Panorama Hotel

44

During the 1930s and World War II as well as during the years leading up to the foundation of the State of Israel, Haifa was the focal point for Jewish immigrants. The port was the destination of ships bearing immigrants and refugees; in fact, it was in Haifa that every second Jewish immigrant first stepped onto Palestinian soil. At the time, the town's Arab population attempted to persuade the British Mandate to take action against the immigrants by instituting a series of strikes.

In 1936 the Palestinian Arabs revolted against the newly founded Jewish settlements as well as against the British mandatory powers which continued to permit the immigration. Britain responded by restricting the immigration and placing strict controls on the purchase of land, which generally resulted in the expulsion of Palestinian tenants.

View of Baha'i Shrine

But the immigration of the Jews continued unabated, supported by the Jewish Agency, which financed the new arrivals, and by the armed *Hagana*, which maintained its headquarters in Haifa. Time and again ships bearing Jewish migrants managed to break through the British blockade. Amongst them was the little *Af-Al-Pi*, which stands today in the grounds of the Museum of Immigration.

Following the founding of the new state of Israel, Haifa (nicknamed the 'Red City' because of its strong labour movement) became the country's largest and most important port. Today, three-quarters of the nation's total imports and exports pass through the vast warehouses and along the quays. Car traffic is a big problem in the centre and the country's major north-south route along the Mediterranean coast passes through the crowded city, causing mile-long traffic jams during the daily rush hours. The town council has plans to alleviate the situation by the year 2000. By then a 6-km (4-mile) tunnel through Mount Carmel should free the town of through traffic.

Sights

Haifa's location made it necessary for many paths over considerable distances to be laid out as steps. Descending the stairways down the side of Mount Carmel gives such a lasting impression of the beauty of the city that the municipal authorities maintain four footpaths (Hebrew: *Madregot*) with particular care. The four signposted paths begin on the mountainside by **Yefe Nof Street** (the terminus of the Carmelit Railway or bus No 22). They lead downhill via more than 1,000 steps past sights, museums and shops and end in the lower town at sea level. Each of the paths affords a magnificent view across the town, the port and the bay.

Cable car, Mount Carmel

Route A (yellow) descends the western slopes of Mount Carmel by means of 1,102 steps, past the Baha'i Shrine to the German Colony. The first half of **Route B** (red) is identical with Route A, but then it branches off at Abbas Street towards the Haifa Museum and ends after a total of 1,021 steps in the Wadi Nisna Quarter. For part of the

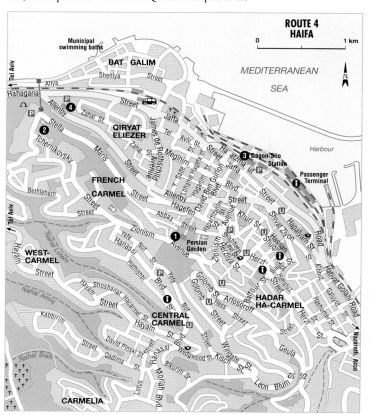

Baha'i Shrine

way, **Route C** (blue) runs parallel to the Carmelit underground railway. It leads directly via 1025 steps to Kikar Paris (Paris Square) below. Finally, **Route D** (green) leads down the eastern slopes of Mount Carmel, crossing the Nordau pedestrian zone and ending 1,034 steps later in the Old City, where some of the buildings date from the 17th and 18th centuries.

Halfway up the slopes of Mount Carmel, in the middle of the magnificent Persian Gardens, stands the ★**Baha'i Shrine** ❶, a temple built by the Baha'i in 1935. Its golden dome, which is visible for miles, is the town's most prominent landmark (daily 9am–12 noon; gardens 8am–5pm).

The Baha'i religion is a monotheistic world religion. It teaches that God has influenced the fate of man through a succession of prophets. Amongst these prophets are Moses, Buddha, Christ and Mohammed. The latest in this line of divine teachers was Baha'ullah, who died in 1892 after 40 years of banishment in exile in Acco. He was buried in his house in Bahji, near Acco. The herald, predecessor and martyr of the Baha'i religion was a Persian who called himself 'Bab', the 'Gateway'. He was executed in 1850 in Tabriz in Iran because his doctrine differed from that of Islam. He lies buried in the magnificent temple shrine in Haifa which was built by his son and successor. The costs of the construction, including the 12,000 golden roof tiles, were donated by the Baha'i communities throughout the world.

Baha'i temple library

Above the shrine stands an equally impressive Baha'i monument, the **Universal House of Righteousness**. It is the highest judicial institution and is responsible for matters of interpretation. Built of white marble, the building boasts 58 Corinthian columns and lies in a beautiful garden which, however, is not open to the public.

During the crusades, many a pious Knight of the Cross settled on the western slopes of Mount Carmel in order to follow in the footsteps of the prophet Elijah and to lead a modest life as a hermit. In 1214 the Catholic Patriarch of Jerusalem granted them the rules of the order '*Ordo fratrum Beatae Mariae Virginis de Monte Carmelo*' (the Order of the Brothers of Our Lady of Mount Carmel). From 1238 the Carmelites, as a contemplative order of mendicant friars, established their monasteries in Europe. Their strict rules of poverty won for them high esteem, especially the branch of 'barefoot Carmelites' who did not even wear shoes. In 1631 Prosper, a simple brother of the barefoot Carmelite order, returned to the mountain on which the order had been founded and built a monastery near the lighthouse. In 1767 the order was forced by Sheikh Dahir el-Omar to give up the buildings.

Carmelite Church

The new monastery buildings were eventually constructed at the foot of Mount Carmel and in 1836 were considerably extended. The **Carmelite Monastery basilica** ❷ (daily 6am–1.30pm and 3pm–6pm), known today as Stella Maris, is impressive, as is a statue of the Virgin whose porcelain head rests on a cedarwood body, and the ceiling frescoes by the monk Luigi Poggi. From the monastery a footpath leads down to the **Cave of Elijah** (Sunday to Thursday 8am–5pm), a grotto 40m (128ft) long and 8m (26ft) wide in which the prophet is to have lived.

47

Cave of Elijah

Haifa possesses more than a dozen museums, including the **Bread Museum** ❸ in Kikar Plumer (guided tours Sunday to Friday 10.30am), the **Railway Museum** in the old Haifa East Railway Station, Kikar Feisal (Sunday, Tuesday, Thursday 10am–12 noon) and the **Museum of Japanese Art** in HaNassi Street (Tuesday to Thursday 10am–12 noon). Particularly impressive is the **National Maritime Museum** ❹ in Allenby Street (Sunday to Thursday 10am–4pm, Saturday 10am–1pm). Founded in 1953 as the private collection of the Israeli frigate captain Arie L. Ben-Eli, who directed the museum until his death in 1980, it is today one of the few specialist museums in the Mediterranean area which is dedicated to the 5,000-year-old history of navigation.

Amongst the exhibits are models of the 'Tarshish' ships which sailed the seas 1,000 years before Christ during the reign of King Solomon; Egyptian funeral barges from the second millennium before Christ; a variety of nautical instruments from down the ages; ancient charts; and a section containing some 1,000 amphora, the oldest of which date from the Bronze Age.

Directly beneath the Maritime Museum lies the **Clandestine Immigration and Naval Museum** (Sunday to Thursday 9am–4pm, Friday until 1pm).

Bathing at the lake, Tiberias

Sailing is popular

Route 5

★Tiberias and the Sea of Galilee

Nobody travels to Tiberias because of its outstanding sights, but rather because of its impressive location on the Sea of Galilee. By day visitors can enjoy a view far across the lake to Mount Hermon and across to Golan, and by night the villages and kibbutzim along the shores form a glittering necklace of light. Tiberias, a town with 40,000 inhabitants, is famous for its hot springs, whose healing properties were described in glowing terms by the Roman-Jewish historian Flavius Josephus.

History

Tiberias, which lies 200m (640ft below sea level, was founded in the year 18AD by Herod Antipas, the son of Herod the Great, on the ruins of the Canaanite town of Rakkat. It was named in honour of the Emperor Tiberias, the ruler of the Roman Empire at the time.

After the destruction of the Second Temple and the expulsion of the Jews from Jerusalem, many Jewish scholars settled in Tiberias and founded rabbinical academies here. Thus during the 2nd century the town became the centre of Jewish learning in Palestine. The Sanhedrin, the High Council and Jewish Court of Justice, had its seat here, and the Mishna, the most important collection of Jewish precepts handed down by oral tradition, was completed here. For this reason, Tiberias is considered to be one of the four holy cities of Judaism.

In 1099 the Norman Crusader Tancred proclaimed himself Prince of Galilee and founded the modern town north of the Roman settlement. It remained the headquarters of the Knights of the Cross in Galilee until 1247, when it was badly damaged. It was not until the 16th century that Jews expelled from Spain rebuilt the town.

The Zionist immigration during the first half of the 20th century increased the Jewish percentage of the population, and the kibbutzim founded at the same time in the vicinity increased the region's prosperity. Since 1948 the population of Tiberias has been almost entirely Jewish.

Sights

The most prominent landmarks of Hamat Tiberias, the oldest and southernmost part of the town, are the white domes of the **Synagogue** (Eliazar Kaplan Road), which houses the tomb of the revered Rabbi Meir. Meir was a scholar whose nickname was *Baal Haness*, the 'Miracle Worker', and to this day his tomb is a place of pilgrimage for many Jews. Rabbi Akiva, who was put to death by the Romans after the Bar-Kochba Uprising, and the medieval Jewish historian Rabbi Rambam, who died in 1204, were two other scholars who died in Tiberias and whose tombs are treated with great reverence by the Jewish people (Trumpeldor Street and Yohanan Ben Zakkay Street).

The principal sight in Tiberias is the **Archaeological Park**. Excavations in the vicinity of the Jordan River Hotel revealed the remains of a Crusaders' church, town walls dating from the Byzantine era and the ruins of a synagogue with particularly fine mosaic floors. The site was declared a national monument and transformed into an open-air museum (Sunday to Thursday 10am–12 noon and 3pm–5pm).

Today the **Municipal Museum** is housed in the former mosque **Jami El-Bahri** directly on the shores of the lake. Palestinian fishermen used to sail right up to the mosque in order to attend to their daily prayers. Since the construction of the new promenade the mosque now stands a little further inland, behind the yachting marina.

The town's main tourist attraction is the new **Lakeshore Promenade** (Tayyelet), which is 500m long. It bustles with activity from early morning until late at night: street artists, musicians, craftsmen's stalls, strolling passers-by, crowded cafés – and the view across the Sea of Galilee towards Golan.

Round the Sea of Galilee

Those wishing to follow in the footsteps of Jesus and to discover Biblical history by the Sea of Galilee (Lake Tiberias) (Hebrew: Yam Kinnereth), should travel by bicycle, car or bus to the villages on the lake's northwest shore not served by the ferry from Tiberias to Ein Gev.

It was on the shores of the lake that the historical Jesus actually lived, taught and healed the sick. Along the lakeshore, where fishermen still throw out their nets, His

Roman ruins **49**

A dangerous descent

first disciples abandoned theirs to follow Him: Simon Peter and his brother Andrew, and the brothers James and John.

The sign on the outskirts of **Magdala**, a few miles north of Tiberias, recalls the home of Mary, called Magdalene, a Galilean woman who accompanied Jesus and His disciples. Further inland lies the moshav **Migdal**.

A gently rounded mountain peak beyond the road skirting the northern shore of the lake is known as the Mount of the Beatitudes, where Jesus preached the Sermon on the Mount. Today the slope is crowned by the **Church of the Beatitudes**, a domed building dating from 1937 with a peristyle affording a magnificent view across the lake.

House of St Peter, Capernaum

In **Capernaum** (Kfar Nachum), which lies directly on the north shore of the lake, archaeologists have unearthed a large number of finds in the course of their excavations. These include a synagogue dating from the 3rd century with Corinthian colonnades. Not far from here lies **Tabgha**, the Greek Heptapegon ('Seven Springs'). Since the 4th century this has been regarded as the place where Jesus fed the five thousand.

On the northernmost point of the lake, the River Jordan flows into the Sea of Galilee. At this stage it is not a vast, surging river, but rather a wide, gently flowing stream. A small one-track bridge suffices to cross to the other side. Continuing down the eastern shore of the lake, the route runs through a region below the Golan Heights which before 1967 belonged to Syria. Passing through the new holiday village of **Kinar**, the road eventually arrives in **Ein Gev**, which lies exactly opposite Tiberias, and which is the best known agricultural kibbutz in the region. However, its spacious holiday village, campsite and the breeding of John Dory fish add more to the income of the kibbutz families than their fruit and vegetable plantations.

Kibbutznik barbecue

The success of Ein Gev as a holiday resort has resulted in the construction of more holiday villages further south along the eastern lakeshore: **Haon** and **Maagan** are both popular family destinations. The point where the Jordan flows out of the lake again is an area of intensive farming. After another 8km (5 miles) the road returns past the new International Health and Recreation Centre to enter Hamat Tiberias once more.

The Sea of Galilee

A detour to Nazareth

Only half an hour's drive (37km/23 miles) from the places where Jesus preached around the Sea of Galilee lies the little town where his parents Mary and Joseph lived. It was in Nazareth that the Archangel Gabriel announced Jesus's birth (Luke 1,31), it was here that he spent his youth (Luke 2,40), and it was from Nazareth that Jesus was driven away

Nazareth from the hills

when he began to preach (Luke 4,28). Travellers who opt for the somewhat longer approach via Afula, setting out from Bet Yerah to the south of Tiberias, can stop halfway to climb **Mount Tabor**. The mountain, which is 588m (1,882ft high), can be seen for miles around. It is regarded as being the Mount of the Transfiguration (Luke 9,28). The winding road leading to the mountain begins in the village of Labburiya.

★ **Nazareth**, with its population of 60,000, is the largest Arab town in Israel. It contains many sites recalling events in the life of the Holy Family. The most important amongst them all is the **Basilica of the Annunciation**, completed by the Italian architect Giovanni Muzio in 1969. Built of marble with a cone-shaped cupola, it is also the largest church in the Middle East (daily 8am–noon, 4–6pm). The church marks the spot where the Archangel Gabriel is supposed to have informed the Virgin Mary that God had chosen her to bear his son. The event is depicted inside by elaborate murals, each from a different country; Mary appears variously in a kimono, a turban and in cubist style.

Some of the simpler churches in Nazareth capture an air of intimacy and sanctity that the colossal basilica lacks. This is especially so in the Greek Orthodox **Church of St Gabriel**. The only sound to be heard upon entering the church is the faint rush of water; lapping against the sides of the old well is the same underground spring that provided Nazareth with its water 2,000 years ago. It takes only a little imagination to envision the scene described in the Gospels when 'Mary took the pitcher and went forth to fill it with water' – at which point the angel Gabriel is said to have descended and informed her of the surprising news.

In the basement of the **Church of St Joseph** (next to the Basilica), is a cavern said to have been the carpentry workshop of Joseph.

Monk at the Basilica of the Annunciation

51

Church of St Gabriel

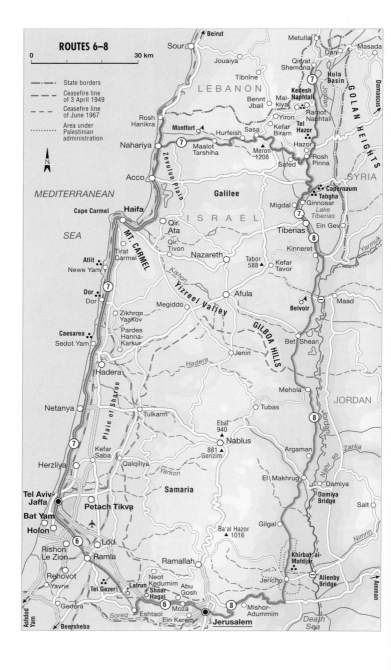

ROUTES 6–8

0   30 km

State borders
Ceasefire line
of 3 April 1949
Ceasefire line
of June 1967
Area under
Palestinian
administration

N

Beirut
Sour
Jouaiya
Tibnine
LEBANON
Metulla
Masada
Qiryat
Shemona
Dan
⑦
Hula
Basin

GOLAN HEIGHTS

Damascus

Rosh
Hanikra
Montfort
Hurfeish
Sasa
Bennt
Jbail
Mal-
kiya
Yiron
Kefar
Biram
Kedesh
Naphtali
Ramot
Naphtali
Tel
Hazor
Nahariya
⑦
Maalot
Tarshiha
Meron
~1208
Hazor
Rosh
Pinna
SYRIA

Acco
Galilee
Safed

MEDITERRANEAN
Cape Carmel
Haifa
Qir.
Ata
ISRAEL
Capernaum
Tabgha
Migdal
Ginnosar
Lake
Tiberias
Ein Gev

SEA
MT. CARMEL
Qir.
Tivon
Nazareth
⑦
Tiberias
⑧
Kinneret

Tirat
Carmel
Tabor
588 ▲
Kefar
Tavor
Yarmuk

Atlit
Newe Yam
Kishon
Afula
Belvoir
Maad

Dor
⑦
Dor
Zikhron
YaaKov
Megiddo
Yizreel Valley
GILBOA
HILLS
Bet Shean

Caesarea
Sedot Yam
Pardes
Hanna-
Karkur
Jenin

JORDAN

Hadera
Hadera
Mehola

Netanya
Tulkarm
Tubas
⑧
Jordan
Zarka

⑦
Kefar
Saba
Ebal
940 ▲
Nablus
Argaman
Nähr es

Herzliya
Qalqiliya
881 ▲
Gerizim
El Makhrug
Damiya

Yarkon
Samaria
Damiya
Bridge
Salt

Tel Aviv-
Jaffa
Petach Tikva
Gilgal
Nimrin

Bat Yam
Holon
Ba'al Hazor
▲ 1016
Khirbat
al-
Mafdjar

⑥
Lod
Ramallah
Jericho
Allenby
Bridge
Amman

Rishon
Le Zion
Ramla
Neot
Kedumim
Abu
Gosh

Rehovot
Yavne
Tel Gezer
Latrun
Shaar
Hagai
⑥
Moza
⑧
Mishor-
Adummim
Death
Sea

Gedera
Soreq
Eshtaol
Ein Kerem
Jerusalem

Ashdod
Yam
Beersheba

52

Route 6

From Tel Aviv to Jerusalem

★ Tel Aviv – ★ Neot Kedumim – ★ Abu Gosh –
★★★ Jerusalem (78km/49 miles)

There are a number of interesting sights worth a short stopover lying off the National Highway No 1 between Tel Aviv and Jerusalem. The 80-km (50-mile) stretch of highway, for which you should allow an entire day, is redolent with tradition. Here you will discover an unexpected side of Israel's character: the 'green archaeology' of Biblical Palestine in Neot Kedumim or the colourful history of the Arab hamlet of Abu Gosh.

Jerusalem lies at an altitude of 800m (2,560ft) in the mountains of Judea. The early pilgrims took more than a week to make the journey from the port of Jaffa through the foothills to the Holy City. Today the trip by train takes about two hours, with departures twice a day. The uphill route through the limestone gorges of the Sorek Valley beyond Beth Shimesh is spectacular, and the trains are mostly full. Alternatively, the entire journey can also be made by Egged bus or Sherut taxi.

Leaving ★ **Tel Aviv** (*see page 33*) on National Highway No 1 towards Lod, turn off to the east along District Road No 443 near Ben Shemen, a moshav founded in 1921. Continue towards the settlement of **Modiin**, birthplace of the Hasmonean family, leaders of the great 2nd-century BC revolt against the Syrian-Greek empire which controlled Judea. The revolt started when the villagers were ordered to sacrifice a cockerel on a pagan altar; led by

53

Pointing the way
The River Jordan valley

Judas Maccabeus, it rapidly spread all over Judea, resulting in the recapture of the temple and the restoration of Jewish worship in Jerusalem. Not much remains of ancient Modiin, but an attractive park has been laid out with a model of a village of the period of the revolt.

On the left after about 4km (2½ miles) lies ★ **Neot Kedumim** (42km/26 miles), the 'Oasis of the Old' (Sunday to Thursday 8.30am–sunset, Friday 8.30am–1pm; last admissions two hours before closing time; guided tours Tuesday and Friday 9.30am in winter and 3.30pm in summer). It is planned to recreate the natural surroundings of the Bible in this, 'the World's Only Biblical Landscape Reserve'. Of the more than 100 plants, trees and flowers named in the Five Books of Moses, fewer than one-third are still extant in Israel today. 'God's language is plants, animals and stones' proclaims a sign in the Biblical landscape park. Along the three signposted footpaths there are signs with explanations, and free guided tours in English are also available.

Just to the north of the French Trappist **Monastery of Latrun** is **Canada Park**, a recreation centre with vineyards, almond orchards, ancient fig trees and adventure playgrounds. In the park are the ruins of a village thought to be the Emmaeus of the New Testament, where the risen Jesus was seen, according to St Luke's gospel.

Continuing along the National Road No 1, the route passes through the so-called **Martyrs' Forest**. Clothing the slopes of the Judean foothills, 100,000 trees are planted here in memory of the 6 million Jews who were murdered during the Holocaust. On the right-hand side of the road lie the rusting wrecks of tanks left after the War of Independence; they are freshly painted every year to help keep alive the memory.

★ **Abu Gosh** (63km/39 miles) is a little village which owes its illustrious past to a spring whose water was collected in several cisterns. In the 8th century the Arabs built a caravanserai on the ruins of a Roman military camp. It was destroyed by the Crusaders, who in their turn built a fortified church with an attached monastery named *Castellum Fontenoide*. During the 18th and 19th centuries the Arab villagers of Abu Gosh controlled the road to Jerusalem and extracted a toll from the passing pilgrims. Those reluctant to pay were thrown into the well-preserved Crusader church, which served admirably as a prison. Later the church was purchased and restored by French Benedictine monks. A stone inscription in the church recalls the Tenth Roman Legion, which stopped here in 70AD on its way to Jerusalem.

The route ends after a further 15km (9 miles) in **Jerusalem** (*see pages 18–28*).

54

Date palm

Crusader Church, Abu Gosh

Route 7

Herzliya beach

From the Mediterranean to the heart of Galilee

★ Tel Aviv – Herzliya – ★★ Caesarea – ★ Haifa –
★★ Acco – ★ Safed – Jordan Springs – ★ Tiberias
(241km/151 miles)

55

The journey from the Mediterranean coast of Israel to
the heart of Galilee runs past long, broad, sandy beaches
and modern seaside resorts before arriving in Caesarea,
with its Roman remains, and Haifa, the country's largest
port and at the same time one of its loveliest towns. In Acco
you will discover buildings left behind by the Crusaders,
and in Safed the Jewish cabbala tradition. Finally, in
Tiberias and by the Sea of Galilee you will find the places
where Jesus lived and preached. The journey will take
about three to four days; it is advisable to plan overnight
stops in Haifa and Safed.

The main road which runs parallel to the coast is of
motorway standard. Running alongside it further inland
is a second main road from Petach Tikva to Hadera, from
where a minor road continues directly to Haifa. Those who
prefer not to drive can take the train, whose route runs
between the two roads; further north, it follows the con-
tours of the coast. Sea views to the west and, to the east,
vistas across the fertile fields and orchards of the Plain
of Sharon accompany the traveller. Further north the low-
lands give way to the foothills of Mount Carmel.

On the beach

Leaving Tel Aviv in a northerly direction and crossing the
Yarkon River, the route continues across the northern Plain
of Sharon before entering **Herzliya** (15km/9 miles). Even
in olden times, the Plain of Sharon promised rich harvests.
For this reason, it was here that immigrant Jews from the

Sunning at Herzliya

Paragliding at Netanya

US with the assistance of the Jewish Agency founded a village north of Tel Aviv, naming it Herzliya in memory of Theodor Herzl. It soon expanded to become the heart of the orange- and lemon-producing region. Industrial developments were added, and after the founding of Israel it was not long before local businessmen became aware of the advantages of the fine, long sandy beach for the development of the tourist industry.

Today Herzliya has a population of 100,000 and belongs to the Tel Aviv catchment area. During the week, the gently sloping beach becomes the playground of the guests of the three luxury hotels spaced out at a respectful distance from one another beyond the shore. At weekends, it is the turn of the citizens from Tel Aviv. An insight into the history of the settlement is provided by the **Beit Rishonim Museum**, a house belonging to one of the oldest families in town set in a lovely garden (Rehov Hanadiv, Sunday to Thursday 10am–noon and 3pm–5pm).

Continuing along the main road in a northerly direction, you will soon reach **Netanya** (32km/20 miles). Founded in 1929, the self-styled 'Pearl of the Plain of Sharon' proudly underlines its central location at the heart of Israel's corn growing area as well as its importance as a market town for the agricultural products produced in the surrounding region. Today, however, the main source of income is no longer citrus fruits, but tourists. The seemingly endless beach of golden sand provides ideal conditions. Netanya is a lively seaside resort, the loudest and largest on Israel's Mediterranean coast. It boasts a long beachfront promenade, plenty of cafés, exemplary sports facilities by land and sea and a better selection of good hotels than any of the country's other resorts with the exception of Eilat.

During World War II, Jewish families from the German-occupied Netherlands came to settle in Netanya. With them they brought their skills in the cutting and polishing of diamonds. Today the second generation has made Netanya the most important diamond centre in Israel.

★★Caesarea

Situated halfway between Tel Aviv and Haifa, 15km (9 miles) north of Netanya, **Caesarea** (47km/29 miles) has the most important archaeological excavations on the Mediterranean coast of Israel. Following the plans of Herod the Great, construction of Caesarea began two decades before the birth of Christ. The town was named in honour of the Roman emperor Caesar Augustus,

Caesarea's amphitheatre

and it was intended that the town should lack none of the attributes associated with the Graeco-Roman culture of the time. As many as 20,000 spectators could enjoy the spectacle of horse and chariot racing in the Hippodrome on a 230-metre long track. Larger-than-life marble statues adorned the Forum. The theatre, with a capacity of 10,000 seats and a situation directly by the coast, claimed to have the best acoustics of any in the land. In order to guarantee the links with Rome, Herod went to great lengths to compensate for the lack of a natural harbour by building an artificial marina with docks, warehouses and a lighthouse. Thanks to its breakwater, it later became the most important anchorage on the Palestinian coast. Following the quelling of the Jewish uprising which had led to the destruction of the Temple in AD70, Caesarea became the capital of the Roman province. St Paul the Apostle spent several days as a prisoner in the local jail before he was deported to Rome.

Not much of the magnificence of the Roman town has survived to this day. The existence of the **Hippodrome [A]** can be deduced from a green hump, and of the former **Forum** all that remains are two statues in fair condition. Only two monuments are sufficiently well maintained to merit a visit. In the south of the town lies the **Theatre [B]**, which was restored in 1961. Its 100-metre-wide stage forms the scene during the summer months of spectacular open-air performances. In 1993 Verdi's *Aida* was 'imported' from Verona and played for weeks to packed audiences. Finally, the **Aqueduct [C]**, in the north of the town, supplied the Caesarea of ancient times with water from the northeast Carmel mountains.

In 1101 the Crusaders conquered Caesarea for the first time. In 1187 they lost it again to Sultan Saladin, but returned in 1191 under Richard the Lionheart. In 1265 they finally had to surrender to Sultan Beibar. Under their rule,

Archaeologists in the old Crusader city

Caesarea: the new...
...and the old

Shopping gallery sculpture

the harbour, which had fallen into decay and had silted up, was made navigable again and a **Cathedral [D]** was built. It served as the shrine for a relic which was very precious to the Crusaders: a glass dish which had been found in Caesarea and which was revered as the Holy Grail (the historic vessel which Christ used at the Last Supper and in which, according to the legend, Joseph of Arimathea caught the blood of Christ as he hung on the Cross). Excavated sections of this Crusader church and of the ancient port form today the focal point of the **Caesarea National Park** (daily 8am–5pm).

Caesarea has never recovered from its destruction at the hands of Sultan Beibar. Until the founding of the state of Israel, it remained an insignificant Palestinian village. Later, the kibbutz Sedot Yam was founded south of the historic town.

Caesarea is popular amongst sportsmen because of its well-maintained 18-hole golf course. Today it is hard to believe that this was originally laid out in the midst of migrating sand dunes. Greens and fairways as far as the eye can see, shady trees and beds full of brightly coloured flowers have transformed the site into an extensive park which forms a marked contrast to its arid surroundings. The symbol of the Caesarea Golf and Country Club is a Corinthian capital. It was derived from a Roman column which can still be seen on the spot where it was unearthed: in front of the clubhouse in the middle of the golf course.

Until 1993 the remarkable achievements of the engineers who built the town's harbour in Roman times by sinking vast stone blocks into the sea remained invisible. The Mediterranean swell had caused them to sink into the shallow coastal waters over the centuries. With the opening of what is probably the only authentic archaeological underwater museum in the world, some 40,000 sq metres (430,000sq ft) of the sea bed were measured out and 34 sites marked.

A diving school attached to the museum hires out equipment and compressed air. The underwater circuit begins with site No 1. White lines guide the divers to the various archaeological exhibits.

Particularly impressive are the anchors found in the harbour and piled up for the benefit of underwater tourists. At the end of the tour one approaches signpost No 34, which marks the foundations of the ancient lighthouse. It was once 80m (256ft) high and sent out light signals to guide ships towards the harbour entrance. Since trade between Caesarea and Rome was lively in those days, visitors have a good chance of discovering a Roman coin, an oil lamp or perhaps just a piece of ancient pottery.

North of Haifa (98km/ 61 miles) (*see page 43*), the road leads in a gentle curve around the white bay of Haifa. After another 23km (14 miles) you will reach the ancient town of Acco (123km/77 miles).

Acco

Visitors often think of ★★ **Acco** in romantic terms as the city of the Crusaders. Indeed, when you gaze at the Gothic churches and medieval castles with which the Knights of the Cross adorned the Holy Land, it is easy to forget the historical background, which belonged to one of the darkest chapters of European history.

Spice stall in the Old City

The crusades were initiated as a result of rumours that the Holy Sepulchre had fallen into the hands of infidels. This was not true, for the Christian places of worship in Palestine had been controlled by Christians for centuries, albeit followers of the Byzantine-Orthodox faith and not of Catholicism. The schism in 1054 marked the final break with Rome. By 1098, however, Palestine was firmly in hands of the Islamic Fatimids from Egypt, and there was no longer any need to 'liberate' the holy places.

Nonetheless, preparations for the crusades continued, accompanied by anti-Jewish pogroms in Europe. It was hoped to turn the campaigns to financial advantage through the opening of new trade routes, and the Italian mercantile republics provided massive support for the Crusader armies. In 1099 they conquered Jerusalem, massacring thousands of Jews and Muslims, and in 1100 Baldwin I had himself crowned King of Jerusalem, conquering Ashkelon, Haifa and Acco during the same year. By 1115 the whole of Palestine and large parts of what is now Jordan and Syria belonged to the Kingdom of Jerusalem.

Off to school in Acco

The kingdom had a feudal structure. Fiefs were given to noble families, knightly orders and the Church, whilst the crown retained large areas of land for itself. For almost

Restaurant on Old City wall

Old fishing harbour, Acco

a century the Catholic Knights – mostly French and Italian – secured their kingdom by building churches, monasteries and fortresses. Then in 1187 Sultan Saladin won the first victory over the Crusaders in Hittim in Galilee.

In 1191, the Third Crusade, under Richard the Lionheart and Frederick Barbarossa, succeeded in regaining possession of the coastal strip between Jaffa and Tyre 'for Christianity'. Jerusalem remained under Muslim rule, and so Acco was declared the capital of the knights' kingdom.

The Fourth Crusade ended with the plundering of Constantinople; the armies of the Fifth were soundly beaten by the Egyptians. The Sixth Crusade ended in 1228 with negotiations with the Egyptian rulers of Jerusalem and the re-establishment of the Kingdom of Jerusalem more or less within its old boundaries under Emperor Frederick II of Hohenstaufen.

However, strife between the Christian noblemen opened the way for the Mameluke sultans of Egypt to invade the country. By 1271 Acco had become the last bastion of the Knights of the Cross in Palestine, and 20 years later the final fall of the city to the Muslims marked the end of a 200-year epoch.

For all its Christian past, the 4,000-year-old town has retained to this day its Arab-oriental character. It can be felt especially in the narrow alleys of the Old City, in the bazaars near the harbour, despite the fact that these days there are usually more small yachts than fishing boats tied up at the quays.

History

Over the millennia, Acco changed its name several times. Its first official mention as a fortified port occurs in the so-called Egyptian Execration Tablet dating from the 19th century BC. Later, in the 7th century BC, Assyrian documents testify to the diligence of its Phoenician inhabitants. After its conquest by Alexander the Great in 333BC, Acco also became subject to Greek influence. In honour of the Diadochus Ptolemy II Philadelphus, who lived in Egypt, the city was renamed Ptolemais. It was known by this name in the Bible: 'And when we had finished our course from Tyre, we came to Ptolemais, and saluted the brethren, and abode with them one day,' as St Paul describes the end of his Greek journey (Acts 21, 7).

Before that the Romans had declared the town to be a Roman colony and under the Emperor Nero had changed its name to Colonia Claudia Ptolemais. It was not until after the Islamic conquest of the Middle East during the 7th century AD that the town reverted to its original name once more – but only until 1104, five years after the fall of Jerusalem, when it was forced to surrender to the Crusaders for the first time. After Sultan Saladin had reconquered the town once more in 1187 and the flag of the Prophet had fluttered from the battlements for four long years, the Crusaders took Acco again in 1191. This time they re-christened the town Saint-Jeanne d'Acre. After Saladin had conquered Jerusalem in 1187, Acco was the last town in the Kingdom of Jerusalem to be held by the Crusaders. At one stage Saint-Jeanne d'Acre had a population of 40,000. It became the regional trading headquarters of both the Genoese and the Venetians. Their monopoly over the trading fleet enabled them to transfer the entire supplies for the Crusaders through the ports of their native trading republics.

In the long term, however, Acco could not withstand the attacks of the Muslim armies. In 1271 Sultan Beibar drove the Knights of the Cross out of Montfort fortress, and in 1291 Saint-Jeanne d'Acre was the last bastion in the Holy Land to fall to the Muslims.

With the end of the Age of the Crusades, Acco sank into oblivion for 500 years, although under Turkish rule it remained a provincial capital and thus the seat of government of the Pashas.

From 1775, the town rose to new glory under Ahmad Pasha al-Jazzar ('The Butcher'), notorious for his cruelty. He surrounded the Old City with a wall; visitors can still stroll along the battlements to this day. He also fortified the town to such an extent that it was even able to withstand a two-month siege by the armies of Napoleon.

61

Sights

Today, what impresses visitors to Acco most are the buildings dating from the 200 years when it was a Crusader stronghold. The ★★ **Crusaders' City** ❶ (daily 9am–5pm, Friday 9am–1pm) lies in some places as much as 10m (32ft) below street level. The tour includes the **Chapter**

A card game hots up

Eating out in Acco

Khan-el-Umdan

Al-Jazzar Mosque

Room which, with its massive round columns and impressive early Gothic cross vaulting, transports the visitor back into the age of chivalry. The same applies to the **Crypt**, the magnificent refectory and ceremonial hall of the Knights of St John, in which Marco Polo is also said to have been a guest. The Crusaders' City can be entered through the **Citadel**, a fortress dating from the time of Ahmad al-Jazzar. The exit is at the end of a 65-m (208-ft) long tunnel in the *Domus infirmorum*, the hospital of the Knights of St John, popularly known as the 'Bosta'.

Ahmad Pasha al-Jazzar also built the ★ **Al-Jazzar Mosque ❷** which bears his name and which serves as shrine for three hairs of the Prophet Mohammed (Saturday to Thursday 8am–6pm except at prayer times). He was also responsible for the construction of the **Khan el-Umdan ❸**, the 'Pillar Caravanserai'. The massive two-storey building forms a square around an enclosed courtyard framed by attractive rounded arches. In the very centre there once stood a well. The caravanserai provided adequate accommodation for travelling merchants and their camels.

Nahariya (154km/96 miles) lies 10km (6 miles) north of Acco. German Jews settled here in 1934 around the mouth of the River Gaaton. Before emigrating, they had decided to abandon their previous careers, most of which had been of an academic of commercial nature, and to earn their living henceforth as farmers. Since then the little agricultural community has developed into an attractive seaside resort which emphasises its tranquil and relaxing atmosphere. Of course, Nahariya also has plenty of entertainment to offer, and for those who lay store by such

amenities, its long sandy beach also boasts a good infra-structure. Nonetheless, everything here is simply smaller than in the big resorts further south. The town's main axis is formed by the eucalyptus-fringed **Ha Gaaton Boulevard**. It runs from east to west parallel to the river of the same name, ending by the beach at a point where the surf makes the sea particularly attractive for bathing.

A few kilometres south of Nahariya lies Shave Zion, an agricultural settlement (moshav) whose main sight is the impressive mosaic floor of a Byzantine church dating from the 4th century. A small roofed memorial at the entrance to the moshav recalls that it was founded in 1938 by Jews from the Black Forest. Shave Zion lies directly on the coast and is ideal for a refreshing break. From here it is possi-ble to travel to the white cliffs of ★ **Rosh Hanikra** ('The Cape of Caves') on the Lebanese border.

Rosh Hanikra

From Nahariya, National Highway No 89 leads in an easterly direction inland towards the Biblical region of **Galilee** (Hebrew: Ha Galil). It is gently rolling hilly coun-try between the Mediterranean and the Jordan. Here, in the north, the Crusaders built one of their most impos-ing fortresses. To visit it, turn off in a northerly direction in the little village of **Miilya**, 17km (11 miles) east of Na-hariya. ★ **Montfort** was built as part of the defences of Acco by Hermann von Salza and his Teutonic Order. Orig-inally named 'Starkenburg Fortress', the castle surren-dered in 1271 to Sultan Beibar without a struggle. For this reason it is still in good condition, although some sections have collapsed over the past 700 years.

63

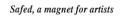

White cliffs at Hanikra

To the right of the road above Sasa stands **Mount Meron**, at 1,200m (3,820ft) the highest peak in Galilee. ★ **Safed** (206km/129 miles), the 'Town of Synagogues', lies 850m (2,720ft) above sea level, which makes it one of the high-est towns in the Holy Land.

Safed, a magnet for artists

After the departure of the Crusaders, who in 1102 had erected the fortress of **Mezuda** which can be seen for miles around, Safed became home to a flourishing Jewish com-munity. At the end of the 15th century, the town's grow-ing prosperity attracted a large number of the Jews who had been forced to leave Spain by the Inquisition. Dur-ing the 16th century Safed had the highest proportion of Jewish inhabitants of any town in the country, including large numbers of scholars and rabbis whose writings played an important part in the preservation of the Jew-ish faith. Safed was the centre of Jewish mysticism, of the cabbala, and became one of the four holy places of Judaism. The tombs of the cabbalistic scholars are still im-portant places of pilgrimage.

Safed also possessed an Arab tradition which, however, has left few traces behind. During the War of Indepen-

War memorials, Qiryat Shemona

The disputed Golan Heights

Skiing on the Golan Heights

dence in 1948 the Palestinians were driven out of Safed. Artists of all types settled in the former Arab quarter, and so today in the **Hazayarim** district of town you will encounter large numbers of painters and sculptors offering their paintings, sculptures, stone carvings or metal objects for sale.

From Safed, the road winds in steep bends eastwards as far as **Rosh Pina** (7km/4 miles), a small village on the edge of the Jordan Valley with the only airport in the north of the country. From here a detour to the north leads to Qiryat Shemona, 30km (19 miles) away. On the right-hand side of the road, stretching away towards the Jordan, lie the lakes and marshes of the **Hule Valley Nature Conservation Area** (*see page 8*).

Qiryat Shemona (20,000 inhabitants) was founded in 1950 for new immigrants. This town on the Lebanese border lies in a narrow but fertile valley. Its name, 'The Town of the Eight', harks back to the pugnacious Zionist Trumpeldor. He was killed in nearby Tel Hai in 1920, together with his companions. Today the town is characterised by the textile and metal industries brought by the new settlers.

Eight kilometres (5 miles) east of Qiryat Shemona lies the ★ **Dan Nature Conservancy Area,** in which lies the source of the Dan, one of the three principal tributaries of the Jordan. Narrow paths lead through the protected area, which is covered by varied vegetation with dense tree and bamboo groves. In the course of a circuit you will cross several tributary streams of the Dan; their ice-cold waters make the steamy heat of the forest more bearable, especially in summer.

On the way back from Qiryat Shemona to Rosh Pina the traveller is accompanied to the east by the impressive **Golan Heights**. The Golan forms a high-altitude plateau which runs east of the Jordan over a distance of some 75km (47 miles) from the heights of Mount Hermon on the Syrian-Lebanese border to the Yarmuk River in the south.

Before 1967, from these Golan Heights, Syria controlled the region around the Hule Valley and the eastern shore of the Sea of Galilee. In 1967 Israel conquered the Heights, later annexing them and adopting an aggressive settlement policy. United Nations troops observed the truce in the region from 1967, but by 1995 Israel was prepared to discuss the Golan's future with Syria.

It is possible to visit the Golan Heights either from Quiryat Shemona or from Rosh Pina. Further south along the main road, after another 10km (6 miles), the route descends to the Sea of Galilee and shortly thereafter to the town of **Tiberias** (241km/151 miles) (*see page 48*).

Route 8

From Tiberias to Jerusalem

★ Tiberias – ★ Bet Shean – Nablus (detour) – ★★ Jericho – Wadi Qelt (detour) – ★★★ Jerusalem (145km/ 91 miles)

Making the desert bloom

This full-day excursion is full of variety. It begins amongst the green plantations by the Sea of Galilee, 200m (640ft) below sea level. It leads through arid landscapes along the Jordan Valley via Bet Shean to Jericho, the capital of the new Palestinian state, and finally climbs through steep hairpin bends up to Jerusalem, 1,000m (3,200ft) higher up. The easiest way of making the trip is in a rented car. The alternative is to take the bus with stops in Bet Shean and Jericho.

From ★Tiberias (*see page 48*) the route follows the Sea of Galilee in a southeasterly direction. At the beginning of this century the southern shores of the lake formed a popular destination for Jewish immigrants. Here they founded their first kibbutzim and began to cultivate the land, transforming the region into a fertile area for the production of fruit and vegetables of every kind.

A few kilometres south of the point where the River Jordan leaves the Sea of Galilee lies the kibbutz of **Deganya**. Founded in 1909, it is the oldest in the country. The scientific institute which forms part of the kibbutz owns a collection of 30,000 books on the nature and history of Palestine. It is named after Aaron Gordon, one of the founding fathers (Sunday to Thursday 9am–4pm).

The further one travels southwards away from the lake, the more arid the scenery becomes. The Jordan (Hebrew: *Hayarden*) soon becomes no more than a meandering

Orange-picking on a kibbutz

brook which has carved for itself a deep bed across the flat plain, whilst the light rock formations and yellow sandy soils of the foothills of the mountains of Samaria characterise the landscape.

A playground for archaeologists

★ **Bet Shean** (35km/ 22 miles) is one of the oldest and most important settlements in the region. 'If Paradise lies in Israel, then Bet Shean is its entrance' – thus the Talmud praises the quality of life in the little town which was mentioned for the first time in Egyptian documents dating from the 19th century BC. In Greek times it was called 'Skythopolis', and under the Romans it was the only town west of the Jordan to be incorporated into the Decapolis League. The Romans left here one of their most magnificent monuments, a **Theatre** with seats for 7,000 spectators which is the best preserved in the region. It forms part of the vast archaeological site which stretches out on the northwest of the present-day town in an area which has been declared a National Park (daily 8am–6pm). Since Skythopolis became a bishopric during the 4th century you will also find in the National Park at the end of an ancient colonnaded street lined with columns the excavated remains of a **Basilica** built 1,500 years ago.

The town was destroyed by an earthquake in 749AD. Bet Shean has never completely recovered. Until the beginning of the 20th century it was just a little Arab village with a few hundred inhabitants known by the name of Beisan. It was not until after the founding of the State of Israel in 1948 that the new town of Bet Shean grew up to the south of the historic city; today the population totals some 25,000.

Ruins of the basilica at Bet Shean

From Bet Shean the route follows a gently curving road southwards. It runs parallel to the Jordan, which is not visible from the road because the river bed forms a deep gorge through the chalky plain. In places, the foothills of the mountains of Samaria extend as far as the road.

Shortly after Argaman, a signpost points the way eastwards to the **Damiya Bridge**. At one time, only Jordanians were permitted to cross the Jordan at this point. Now the bridge is open to all, though it is not recommended to drive through the area with an Israeli licence plate.

At the same junction, however, travellers can make a detour to **Nablus** (70km/44 miles there and back). This Arab town of some 100,000 inhabitants, spread out across the hillside, grew up out of the historic town of Shechem. Today it is the Palestinian headquarters for the northern West Bank, and the centre of the Biblical province of Samaria (Hebrew: Shomeron). It is full of sites with biblical resonance and remains the religious focal point for the Samaritan community; during March and April they celebrate their Pesach festival (Passover) here on the sacred Mount Gerazim.

Nablus

Jericho

Further to the south, the mountains of Samaria retreat and the Jordan valley becomes wider. The landscape, however, remains inhospitable. All the more remarkable, therefore, are the lofty palm trees which suddenly appear on the southern horizon after travelling for another half an hour. Rising above a sea of luxuriant green, they announce the proximity of the oasis of Jericho.

★★ **Jericho** (Arabic: Ar-Riha) (115km/72 miles) lies 270m (864ft) below sea level. Until fairly recently, it was a small Arab town with only 15,000 inhabitants, surrounded by fruit and vegetable plantations, fragrant groves of orange trees and abandoned refugee camps. It had lost its former importance following the Israeli occupation of the West Bank in 1967, and the only visitors who came here were travellers wanting to use the Allenby Bridge, then the only recognised international frontier crossing between Israel and Jordan.

The Gaza-Jericho Accord signed in 1993 between Israel and the PLO transformed Jericho overnight. Today, the Arab coffeehouses along the main street echo with animated discussions about the future of the town which within the terms of this treaty was designated as the seat of the independent Palestinian government.

When Yasser Arafat swore in the members of his government in July 1994, the Palestinian enclave, only 64sq km (24 sq miles) in extent, hardly looked like a 'capital'. But Jericho is a city of great historical importance.

Jericho, the oldest city on earth

Wall portrait of Yasser Arafat

It is regarded by historians as the oldest city in the world. By the **Tell es-Sultan**, north of the town centre, archaeological excavations have revealed a 9-m (29-ft) high tower, originally part of the town fortifications, which dated from the 7th century BC. (Daily 8am–6pm). According to Biblical accounts it was much earlier, during the 13th century BC, that the Israelites under Joshua brought the walls of the city tumbling down with their ram's horn trumpets. The Bible fails to mention that at this time there could have been nothing more to destroy than the dilapidated fortifications of a Canaanite settlement, whose clay bricks have left no trace. In fact, between 3,200 and 1,500BC Jericho was destroyed and then rebuilt at least a dozen times. At this point the traces of the settlement become difficult to follow.

Under the Arabian caliphs, more than 2,000 years later, Jericho rose to fame once more as a regional capital. From this period the magnificently designed **Hisham Palace** (daily 9am–4pm) has survived. It was probably the work of Caliph Hisham's successor El Walid (743–744) who enlisted the help of Byzantine master builders.

Hisham Palace

Jericho's most recent claim to fame is of a more tragic nature. After 1948, its population increased dramatically as a result of the Palestinian refugee camps which grew up on the outskirts of the city. Since 1967, when these same refugees fled for the second time from Israel, the abandoned camps rising up the hillside on the right-hand side of the road have fallen into decay.

It is between Jerusalem and Jericho that the Bible locates the parable of the Good Samaritan (Luke 10, 30-37). 'A certain man went down from Jerusalem to Jericho, and fell among thieves, which stripped him of his raiment, and wounded him, and departed, leaving him half dead. And by chance there came down a certain priest that way: and when he saw him, he passed by on the other side. And likewise a Levite, when he was at the place, came and looked on him, and passed by on the other side. But a certain Samaritan, as he journeyed, came where he was: and when he saw him, he had compassion on him, and went to him, and bound up his wounds, pouring in oil and wine, and set him upon his own beast, and brought him to an inn.'

Wadi Qelt

Since in Biblical times the only link between Jerusalem and Jericho was the **Wadi Qelt**, the story must have taken place here. The ravine, along whose steep walls the Romans had laid aqueducts, remains a popular footpath to this day.

Some 5km (3 miles) west of Jericho is **St George's Monastery** (daily 6am–5pm in summer, 8am–3pm in winter; individual travellers and small groups by prior arrangement), clinging precipitously to the steep north face of the

wadi. Tour guides are fond of comparing it to a swallow's nest. The monastery is the home of Greek Orthodox monks. Its history can be traced back to the 5th century. In those days a number of hermits had chosen the caves in the *wadi* as the ideal location for their silent piety. One of them, John of Thebes, founded the monastery in honour of the Virgin Mary. At the beginning of the 7th century it was the home of Georgios of Choziba, who had been born in Thebes, and after whom the monastery was named following his death in 625. An impressive mosaic floor recalls this era.

St George's Monastery

69

One of the former hermits' caves is dedicated in honour of the prophet Elijah. The monks report that the stream flowing through the Wadi Qelt is the Biblical River Kerit, by which the prophet hid to escape persecution by King Ahab, and where he was fed twice daily by ravens who brought him bread and meat (1 Kings 17).

The natural beauty of Wadi Qelt, the achievement of the architects who built the monastery and the fascinating peace between Jerusalem and the Jordan Valley are an adequate reward for the arduous journey.

Children of Jericho

A fine, modern road leads from Jericho, which lies 270m (864ft) below sea level, to Jerusalem, sitting majestically at an altitude of 800m (2,560ft). A difference in altitude of over 1,000m (3,200ft) must thus be covered over a distance of only 24km (15 miles) from the Jordan Valley to the Mount of Olives.

Twelve km (7½ miles) from Jericho, the driver arrives in front of a signpost indicating the height of sea level. Passing by Mishor Adumim, a dormitory suburb of Jerusalem with an industrial area attached, the road continues through the Arab village of **El-Azariya**, the Bethany of the New Testament, before finally arriving in **Jerusalem** (145km/91 miles).

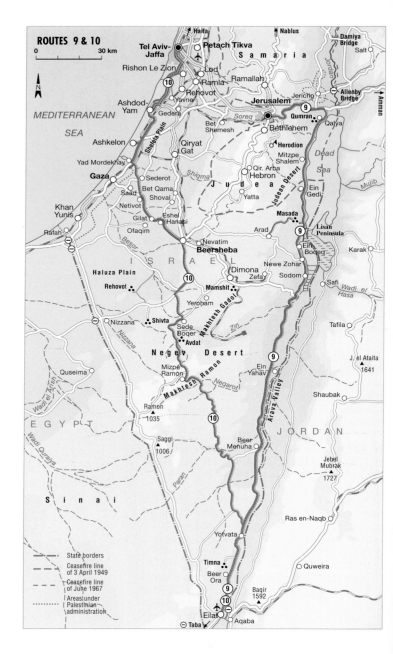

Route 9

From Jerusalem to Eilat

★★★ Jerusalem – ★★★ Dead Sea – Qumran – ★★ Masada – En Boqeq – Sodom – Eilat (307km/ 192 miles)

The route leads downhill from Jerusalem into the Jordan Valley, a difference in altitude of 1,200m (3,840ft). Then it follows the road along the shores of the Dead Sea to the historic towns of Qumran and Masada. Further south again, it crosses the Arava Plain and finally reaches – after climbing over 400m (1,280ft) once more – the seaside resort of Eilat. The journey will take two days, with an overnight stop in Ein Gedi or Ein Boqeq.

From **Jerusalem** (*see pages 18–28*) it is only 30km (19 miles) to the shores of the Dead Sea. Leaving the eastern outskirts of Jerusalem, the Arab suburb of Et Tur, the road winds its way through the rocky gorges of the mountains of Judea. Rusty wrecks of cars by the roadside serve as a constant reminder that the steep descent requires a high degree of concentration. In case of brake failure there are escape ramps at regular intervals. After such an adventurous stretch, drivers are relieved to reach the Jordan Valley at Jericho Junction.

On the right-hand the smooth surface of the ★★★ **Dead Sea** glittering in comes into view. The Dead Sea is one of the most impressive regions in the world. It forms a part of the 5 million-year-old Syrian-African Rift Valley and lies in the deepest section of the Jordan Valley, exactly 394m (1,260ft) below sea level. This inland sea is 85km (53 miles) long and up to 17km (11 miles) wide, and contains more salt and minerals than any other lake on earth.

Beach at the Dead Sea, Ein Gedi

When suntan lotion isn't enough

Every litre of water contains almost 30 percent salt and minerals, more than 10 times as much as normal sea water. The southernmost part of the Dead Sea is divided by the Jordanian Lashon peninsula. Although the northern section is up to 400m (1,280ft) deep; in the south its depth is no more than 10m (32ft). Here, vast clumps of salt float around on the surface, whilst bizarre salt sculptures fringe the shore. The salt is extracted by the 'Dead Sea Works' in vast evaporation basins.

In summer, the temperature around the Dead Sea rises to 48°C/118°F. There are only a dozen days each year on which the sun does not shine. Evaporation is therefore at a very high level and accounts for several million litres a day. For this reason, there is almost always a light haze above the sea. Since the high evaporation rate cannot be balanced out by the Jordan waters which flow into the sea, the Israelis have been planning for years to transfer water from the Mediterranean via a pipeline. A similar plan is described in Theodor Herzl's book *The Jewish State*, published in 1902.

Of course, it is also possible to bathe in the Dead Sea, and what makes the experience exceptional that it is impossible to sink. The water is soft, oily and as warm as a bath. As you lie there motionless in the water, your arms and legs are held up without effort by the upward thrust. Photographs of bathers reading a newspaper while floating in the water are therefore easy to produce. The only way of moving forwards is by paddling like a dog. First-time bathers are always surprised at how hard it is to leave the water: you can't stand up properly until you have almost reached the shore and the water is only knee-deep.

Swimming in the Dead Sea is only recommended at the beach resorts (Enot Zukim near Qumran, Ein Gedi and Hamme Mazor, Ein Boqeq and Neve Zohar at the southern end), where facilities for showering are available.

Healing properties of black mud

Black Mud a natural sediment from the DEAD SEA

Makes you feel young and full of energy, relaxes tensions and soothes pains. Application of Mud stimulates the metabolism and blood circulation. Keeps your skin young and fresh. Can be applied to the entire body, to painful parts, as a beauty face-mask or as a means for strengthening hair growth.

Contents: The solid part (57.6%): Montmorilonite, Caoinite, Ilite, Quartz, Calcite, Feldspare, Organic material.
Liquid part (42.4%): (K/W): Na 3%, K: Cl; Ca 1.23%; Mg 3.32%; Sr 0.03%; I/J: 0.00125; Cl- 18.1%; Mg 0.34%; Hco.-0.29%, Br-0.42%)

Qumran (42km/ 26 miles) lies at the northern end of the west bank of the Dead Sea. Following its destruction by the Romans, very little has remained of the Essenian settlement. Excavations have revealed cisterns, storerooms, houses, a bathhouse, a tower, two potteries and a writing room with stone tables (daily 8.30am–6pm).

Near the ruins stands a modern tourist centre with a comprehensive range of books describing the history and importance of Qumran. It belongs to the neighbouring kibbutz **Qalia**, in whose guesthouse visitors may also spend the night. From the entrance to the archaeological site a footpath leads steeply uphill to the cliffs overlooking the settlement, which are honeycombed with natural caves. It was in these caves, which are numbered nowadays to assist orientation, that the oldest written Biblical texts in the world were found, the *Dead Sea Scrolls*.

A quiet day near Qumran

During the 2nd century BC, the pious Jewish Essenian sect had settled on the northwest coast of the Dead Sea. Its members lived according to ascetic rules, did not marry, had no private fortunes and were highly vocal in their criticism of the religious establishment in Jerusalem. They accused the temple priests in particular of not living according to the rule of God. For 200 years the sect remained in Qumran, until their settlement was destroyed by the Romans in AD68.

Ruins of ancient Essenian building

When it became evident that the Roman army would overwhelm them, the Essenians hid their valuable library, consisting of handwritten scrolls of the Holy Scriptures, religious texts and the rules of the sect, in the inaccessible caves of the surrounding cliffs, in order to save them from the 'unbelieving' Romans. First of all, they wrapped the scrolls in linen and sealed them in clay pots. In the dry atmosphere within the caves, 300m (960ft) below sea level, the treasure remained undiscovered until an Arab shepherd stumbled across it in 1947.

Young Bedouins from the Ta'amira were taking care of their goats on the northwest shore of the Dead Sea when one of the creatures ran away. In the belief that it was hiding in the cave, the shepherds threw stones at the entrance and heard the sound of breaking pottery. Climbing up they found several sealed clay pots containing scrolls covered with writing which they were unable to read. They hoped that someone in nearby Bethlehem would be prepared to buy the scrolls from them, and took their find with them. An Arab antique dealer bought the scrolls and offered them two days later, on 23 November 1947, to Professor L. Sukenik, the archaeologist at the Hebrew University in Jerusalem.

It was at this time that a decision was about to be taken by the United Nations in New York regarding the future of Palestine. Jerusalem and the surrounding region was suffering under conditions resembling civil war. Following difficult negotiations over the purchase price, Sukenik was successful in smuggling three of the scrolls from Bethlehem into the Jewish zone in Jerusalem. They contained half of the Book of Isaiah, texts of the Psalms and a prophetic book describing a war between the Sons of Light and the Sons of Darkness.

In 1954 Sukenik's son, the archaeologist Yigael Yadin, was able to obtain four more scrolls, which had been sold in New York during the War of Independence. This total of seven scrolls, the oldest hand-written Bible texts in the world, and additional finds from the caves of Qumran, are today housed in the Shrine of the Book, a purpose-built section of the Israel Museum in Jerusalem.

Continuing along the road skirting the west bank of the Dead Sea, after some 40km (25 miles) the visitor arrives in the Biblical oasis of **Ein Gedi**, today a kibbutz with an attractive guest house and a health and medicinal cure centre. Only 13km (8 miles) south of Ein Gedi, on the western shores of the Dead Sea, the mighty fortress of ★★**Masada** (Hebrew: Mazada) stands sentinel on a 400-m (1,300-ft) high rocky plateau (Sunday to Thursday 8am–4pm, Friday 8am–2pm). For the citizens of Israel, Masada is as a symbol of their heroic determination to assert themselves. For this reason, until 1985 all recruits in the Israeli army took their oath of allegiance at Masada. 'Masada shall never fall again!' is part of the soldier's oath and the 2,000-year-old inheritance that the Jewish defenders of the stronghold have left behind for all future generations of Israelis since their state was founded. Masada was the setting for the final chapter of the Jewish rebellion against the Romans, which began in 66AD in Caesarea and ended here in 73AD, three years after the destruction of Jerusalem.

Cooling off at Ein Gedi

74

Mighty Masada

The ruins of Masada's fortress

Herod the Great, proclaimed King of the Jews by the Romans, had one of his palaces built on the plateau. The contemporary historian Flavius Josephus reported in his book *The Jewish War* that it was a magnificent edifice: 'The interior furnishings of his rooms, his halls and baths were manifold and splendid. The pillars everywhere were monoliths, the walls and floors adorned with mosaics.' About 70 years after the death of Herod, this fortified palace with its enormous storerooms and granaries became the sanctuary of a group of Jewish zealots, their last bastion, so to speak, after the destruction of Jerusalem. Their heroic resistance lasted for three years. During the last year the Romans built an embankment round the rocky outcrop, and set up eight vast military camps for the 10th Division under their commander Flavius Silva. But because the siege proved fruitless on account of the vast supplies inside the fortress, the Romans took the initiative in an final attack. On the west side they constructed a ramp out of earth and stone blocks, thus enabling them to push their battering rams right up to the gates of the fortress. In view of the inevitable defeat all 960 defenders under their leader El Azar took each other's lives in a mass suicide.

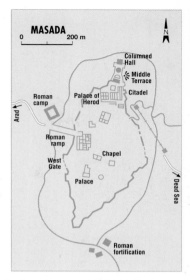

Between 1963 and 1965, Masada was excavated under the guidance of the archaeologist Yigael Yadin and with the help of thousands of volunteers. Masada's highly successful synthesis between reconstruction and leaving things as they were has made it into one of the country's outstanding archaeological sites. Recent research, however, has raised a number of doubts as to whether the historical events as they really happened match the idealised account which has become part of the national myth.

Today there is a cable car up to the plateau. From May until September there are daily *son et lumière* spectacles on the west side, which can be approached from Arad.

View from Masada

Beyond Masada the Lashon (Arabic: *Al Lisan*) peninsula juts out into the Dead Sea. Gazing out across the swimming islands of salt, it becomes clear why this inland sea is known as 'Dead': it houses no living creatures, neither animals nor plants.

Ein Boqeq (104km/65 miles), at the southern end of the Dead Sea, makes a living as a modern spa town and health resort. Nine hotels stand directly on the shore in surroundings utterly devoid of any vegetation; they are the only buildings in Ein Boqeq. The guests have come from all corners of the earth in search of health. For all those

Spa hotel, Ein Boqeq

The Flour Cave, Sodom

Arubotayin Cave

suffering from eczema, psoriasis or severe acne, the Dead Sea succeeds where traditional medicine fails.

At the southern tip of the Dead Sea, 10km (6 miles) past Ein Boqeq, lies **Sodom** (Sedom) (114km/71 miles), a modern town with a peaceful atmosphere. There is no sign of the Canaanite town of the same name, which together with the neighbouring settlement of Gomorrah was cited in the Bible as the very epitome of sinful depravity, hence the origin of the word 'sodomite'. Perhaps this fading into insignificance is the punishment promised by God in the Old Testament.

The **Mountains of Sodom** run parallel to the coast of the Dead Sea over a distance of 10km (6 miles). The mountain chain is composed entirely of salt which has been formed into caves, pillars and canyons by erosion. A particularly prominent pillar which resembles a human figure is known as 'Lot's Wife' in reference to the Old Testament. Lot was a nephew of the patriarch Abraham who succeeded in escaping from Sodom when the city fell. However, his curious wife, who disobeyed the prohibition of the Lord and looked back during their flight, was turned by God into a pillar of salt. Whether Israel's most famous salt pillar will survive the next few millennia as rigid and immovable as before is doubtful. In 1991 a long crack formed in the bottom third, and 'Lot's Wife' slipped more than a foot towards the road below.

South of the Dead Sea the Arava Depression begins. It is the continuation of the Rift Valley running from the Jordan to the Red Sea. After a two-hour car journey along a road framed on either side by the mountain chains of the Negev and Jordan, the traveller arrives in ★ **Eilat** (307km/ 192 miles) (*see pages 38–40*), on the Red Sea. Almost imperceptibly the road has risen 400m (1,280ft) to reach this city at sea level.

Route 10

From Eilat to Tel Aviv

★ Eilat – Mitzpe Ramon – ★ Avdat – ★ Shivta – ★ Beer-sheba – Ashkelon – Ashdod – ★ Tel Aviv (380km/ 238 miles)

The two-day journey from Eilat at the southernmost tip of Israel to Tel Aviv crosses the Negev Desert, through a landscape of bizarre rock formations, arriving in the historic caravan staging post of Beersheba for an overnight stop. Continuing via the ancient towns of Ashkelon and Ashdod on the southern Mediterranean coast, it eventually reaches Tel Aviv.

If you are content with the visual impressions of a desert crossing obtained from a seat in a car or bus, you can easily complete the journey from Eilat to Tel Aviv in a single day (travelling time by Egged bus: six hours), including an unhurried stop in the 'capital' of the Negev, Beersheba. Travellers, however, who wish to experience the wilderness of sand and rock with its gorges and caves, its *wadis*, mountains and craters, who want to feel the burning heat of the sun and smell the *Chamsin*, the hot, sandy desert wind, should allow two days for the Negev. Half-day or whole-day desert tours (5 or 10 hours including meals), night tours by full moon or trips lasting several days are organised from Mitzpe Ramon for small groups travelling by jeep. Prices include food and overnight stops in a sleeping bag under the starry sky.

No place for a breakdown   **77**

When you leave Eilat in a northerly direction, your route passes the copper mines of Timna before entering a magnificent desert landscape.

The Negev Desert occupies the whole of the southern half of the territory belonging to Israel, although only 10 percent of the country's population lives here. The Hebrew name means 'dried out' or 'the dry one', and in fact the southern part of the region has virtually no rain and the northern part less than 300mm (12 inches) a year.

In the west and north, the Negev consists of a relatively flat, dusty plain. In the south, by contrast, limestone, chalk and volcanic granite rocks form impressive mountain chains. Wadis meander through the landscape which has practically no vegetation. If heavy rainfall occurs during the winter months, these dried-out river beds are transformed into raging torrents.

Over the course of millions of years, erosion has resulted in remarkable formations such as the ★ **Makhtesh Ramon crater** which is traversed by highway 40. The best

Ibex at Makhtesh Ramon crater

Roman ruins, Avdat

Crater at Mitzpe Ramon

Modern sculptures, Avdat

Peach-picking, Sede Boqer

view across the crater, which is 300m (960ft) deep, 8km (5 miles) wide and 40km (25 miles) long, can be had from the Visitors' Centre of **Mitzpe Ramon** (153km/96 miles), a desert settlement whose name means in Hebrew 'Ramon's Viewpoint'. It is an apt description. The town was built in 1954 for the workers who constructed the road through the Negev to Eilat.

The western side of the Makhtesh Ramon is dominated by the **Har Ramon**, the highest mountain in the Negev (1,300m/4,160ft).

In ancient times the Nabataeans plied a caravan route straight through the Negev. It linked the Arabian Peninsula with the Mediterranean and led to the growth of the towns of ★ **Avdat** and ★ **Shivta**. The well preserved ruins of the Nabataean temples and tombs, their sophisticated water tanks and well constructions, and the remains of churches and monasteries dating from the 5th century provide evidence of the attempts made to settle in this inhospitable place over the past 2,000 years.

After the founding of the state of Israel, the country's first prime minister, David Ben-Gurion, insisted on the importance of creating new settlements in the Negev. He personally set a good example by taking up residence in the kibbutz **Sede Boqer**, north of Avdat and 40km (25 miles) south of Beersheba, where he spent the last years of his life (he died in 1973).

★ **Beersheba** (268km/168 miles) is today the largest town in the Negev and lies on the northern edge of the desert. The Bible recounts that it was here, near a central oasis, that Abraham made his home. Here it was, too, that God's promise was given, and where the treaty with the Philistine Abimelech took place. Until the 20th century, Beersheba remained a somewhat depressing Bedouin settlement; in

1948 it had no more than 2,000 inhabitants. Then the vast building programmes were instituted whose concrete architecture characterises the town's countenance today. In 1990 the population of the 'University Town of Beersheba' passed the 100,000 mark, and since then their numbers have been increased still further by the arrival of 20,000 'Olim Chadashin', Jewish immigrants from Russia. As in the case of the Israeli settlers after 1948, these new arrivals from Kiev, Minsk and Moscow are to help with the development of new living areas in the Negev.

Every Thursday since 1705, a Bedouin market has been held in Beersheba. The items for sale range from camels to carpets and from jewellery to modern goods.

From Beersheba the journey to Tel Aviv will take approximately 2 hours via the highway No 40.

Continuing via Netivot, the route passes the Gaza Strip to enter **Ashkelon** (334km/209 miles) and the National Park of the same name. The town itself is 3,000 years old and was founded by the Philistines, destroyed by the Babylonians and magnificently rebuilt by Herod. The caliphs extended it, Sultan Saladin conquered it, the Crusaders re-fortified it and in 1270 it was finally completely destroyed by Sultan Beibar. Six centuries later, Ashkelon was used as a stone quarry: when Egyptian weavers settled in the newly founded Majdal (today's Migdal), they used stones from the nearby ruins to build their houses.

Bedouin baking bread, Negev Desert

After 1948 the Arab inhabitants of Majdal fled to the Gaza Strip. The new Israeli settlers changed the name of the town to Migdal. Soon their vast new residential estates had spread to the southern limits of the town, and since 1950 the community, which has grown together to encompass a population of 70,000, bears once more the name of the ancient port. The ruined city in the south of Ashkelon has been declared a National Park; the Roman and medieval buildings are worth seeing, in particular the old port and the town wall, which the Crusaders reinforced by means of dozens of Roman pillars (daily, 8am–5pm). The beaches at **Afridar**, a newer suburb, are fine for bathing.

Ashkelon, however, has ceded its erstwhile importance as a Mediterranean port to **Ashdod** (354km/ 221 miles). Lying only 20km (13 miles) to the north, Ashdod, founded only in 1957, has a burgeoning man-made harbour which has made it the second-most important port in Israel (after Haifa). The town and its surroundings are correspondingly industrialised, and, if not much of a gift to tourism, are a striking example of commercial success. It is also a major immigrant absorption centre.

From Ashdod the motorway leads directly to **Tel Aviv** (380km/208 miles).

Ashdod, an important port

Theatre, Music and the Fine Arts

Israel may be a young country, but its citizens are very active on the cultural front. Eighty out of every 100 Israelis attend a cultural event of some kind each year. According to the statistics published by the United Nations cultural organisation, UNESCO, they thus occupy second place in the world league, second only to the Swiss and well ahead of the British, Germans, Italians and Americans, each of whom can register only a third of this figure on the cultural barometer.

Museums are well attended

Another popular pastime in Israel is visiting museums. Not only does the country boast a large number of important collections – the cities of Jerusalem and Tel Aviv alone total more than 100 between them – but it is also noticeable that the visitors include a high percentage of young people. On late-opening evenings, queues occasionally form in front of some museums, like the Israel Museum in Jerusalem.

Most Israelis also enjoy the theatre – not just entertaining plays, but also controversial works. Israel's drama is almost always politically oriented and demands that its audience form an opinion. Joshua Sobol, the most important contemporary Israeli dramatist, is the embodiment of this trend, and his productions can sometimes be seen on the international stage. Sobol's plays catch exactly the mood and character of his native land. In *Ghetto* he portrays Jews who collaborate with their Nazi persecutors, the main character in *The Palestinian Girl* is maltreated by Israelis, and after one recent work, *The Jerusalem Syndrome*, which blamed Jewish fundamentalists for the situation in the Middle East, the members of the Knesset belonging to the Tehia Party demanded that he kill himself.

Music while you munch

Classical music has as many supporters in Israel as the theatre does. Not only has the country produced a number of famous performers; it also possesses an orchestra with a world-class reputation.

The Israel Philharmonic Orchestra is one of the greatest in the world. Its conductors are so famous that they are often invited to give guest appearances in the principal concert halls of the international music circuit. The orchestra's performances in the Frederic Mann Auditorium in Tel Aviv, their home base, are invariably a sell-out, and subscriptions for the premieres are 'inherited'. Tickets, if available, are only obtainable well in advance. Once a year, usually in May, the Israeli Philharmonic gives a free concert. Hundreds of thousands of music-lovers flock to HaYarkon Park in the north of Tel Aviv.

The fine arts are also of great importance in Israel. Artists' colonies, in which contemporary art is exhibited for sale by the artists themselves in their studios, will be found in El Hod to the south of Haifa, in Safed in Galilee and in Jaffa, the historic district of Tel Aviv. In Jerusalem there is a market specially for art near the Jaffa Gate (Hutzot Hayotzer), around which studios, galleries and shops selling artifacts stand cheek by jowl.

Israel's literature is just as thought-provoking as its drama. Most local writers plead in their works for a closer understanding between Israelis and Palestinians. This is a favourite theme in the writings of Yoram Kaniyuk, one of the country's most popular contemporary authors. It also recurs in the work of Amos Oz, author of the award-winning *Black Box* and *My Michael* and professor of modern Hebrew literature at Ben-Gurion University of the Negev, Beersheba; his work has been translated into 29 languages and he has been a leading figure in the peace movement since 1967's Six-Day War.

The country's other great contemporary authors, Abraham B. Jehoschua and David Grossmann, also tackle the peace theme and analyse with a critical eye political developments. All the works of these writers, however, convey a loving description of Israeli society with undertones of the silent yet ever-present suffering which is the Holocaust's legacy.

Another writer whose longing for peace guides his pen is Uri Averny, who for 10 years was a member of the Israeli parliament. Published in 1950, his book *The Other Side of the Coin* was a bestseller, if a controversial one in Israel, because even then he addressed the subject of the undeniable existence of the Palestinian nation. During the 1980s, in his late work *My Friend the Enemy*, he relates three biographies which indicate his support for the foundation of a Palestinian state. He saw this as the only possibility for Israel's peaceful survival.

Zubin Mehta takes a bow

Festivals

Dance and singing group

Nowadays, the New Year in Israel begins with the New Year Festival *Rosh Hashana* and ends in the month of *Elul* (September/October). Like the Muslim calendar, the Jewish one is based on the lunar cycle. By the introduction of leap months it is possible to fulfill the requirement stated in the Torah that the annual festivals should be adjusted in line with the seasons. (An account of the most important festivals of the Jewish lunar year can be found in Moses 3, 23). For this reason, the Jewish year always begins in the autumn. The calendar and festivals are the expression of a world order which is repeated from year to year. And so, pious Jews still build a shelter of palm leaves – if need be on their balcony for want of a garden – at *Sukkot*, the Festival of Tabernacles, thereby recalling the Return to the Promised Land by symbolically dwelling in it for seven days.

Irrespective of the fact that Israelis have naturally adopted the internationally accepted Gregorian calendar for everyday use and business purposes, the liturgical year and its festivals serve to underline the traditions linking Jews the world over, from American Brooklyn to London or Israel. They all observe the festivals in the same manner: on the first evening of the Passover festival they eat unleavened bread (*matzohs*) and at *Hanukkah* they light the candles of the nine-armed Hanukkah candlestick – adding another each day.

Since all Jewish festivals are also public holidays in Israel, the festivities will be experienced with particular intensity here. Some festivals are serious affairs, such as Rosh Hashana and Yom Kippur; others, such as Pesach (Passover), Shavuot (Feast of Tabernacles) and Succot (Pentecost) are lively festivals of pilgrimage. Yet others

Pilgrims pass the 'Holy Fire' at Easter

are days of remembrance for tragic (Yom Hashoa) or happy events (Yom Haazmaut, Hanukkah and Purim). These festivals can give visitors an insight into an important cornerstone upon which Israeli culture is based.

The official weekly day of rest is the Sabbath, which begins at sunset on Friday and ends 24 hours later. The Muslim day of rest is Friday, a fact which is particularly in evidence in the Jerusalem Old Town and in the Occupied Territories.

The Muslim year is 10 or 11 days shorter than the Gregorian year; this means that the festivals move consistently forward each year by 10 or 11 days. Thanks to the parameters laid down in the Bible, however, the Jewish festivals only vary within relatively narrow monthly limits. The exact dates of the festivals of these two religious groups can be determined only for a limited length of time in advance.

The Purim festival

Three important Jewish festivals occur during the months of September and October: *Rosh Hashana*, the Jewish New Year's Festival (1996: 14–15 September), *Yom Kippur*, the most important Jewish festival ('Day of Atonement'), which achieved tragic fame thoughout the world on account of the Yom Kippur War (1996: 23 September) and, five days later, *Succot*, the seven-day-long Biblical harvest festival, which pious Jews spend in the leafy 'tabernacles' from which the festival gets its name (1996: 28 September–4 November).

85

For eight days in November/December the Jews celebrate *Hanukkah*, the Festival of Light recalling the rededication of the Temple in Jerusalem in 165BC (1996: begins on Thursday 6 December). Large electric lamps are lit outside public buildings and many shops display eight-branched candelabra in their windows.

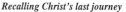

Recalling Christ's last journey

Another historical event, the end of the Babylonian captivity, forms the central theme of the *Purim* festival (1996: 5 March). The same applies to *Pessach* (Passover) (1996: 4 March–11 April), recalling the exodus from Egypt. *Yom Haazmaut* (April/May) celebrates more recent history, for it is the Day of Independence and recalls the foundation of the state on 14 May 1948 (1996: 24 April). Shortly after this (May/June), the Jews return to the distant past. The *Shavuot* festival recalls Moses' revelation of the Ten Commandments (1996: 24 May).

The most important Muslim festivals are the New Year's Festival, the birthday of the Prophet Mohammed *Maulid el-Nabi* (1996: 27 July), *Id el-Fitr*, the festival marking the end of the Ramadan fast (1996: 9 February) and *Id el-Adha* (*Id el-Kebir*), the great sacrificial festival connected with the pilgrimage ceremonies in Mecca and a lively ceremony recalling Abraham's willingness to make a sacrifice (1996: 30 April).

Food and Drink

The biblical residents of the Land of Canaan were nourished by the fertility and abundance of a land 'flowing with milk and honey'. The milk was mainly from sheep and goats, and the honey from dates, figs and carobs. Much depended on the sun, the rains and the seasons. Food was simple; feast predictably followed famine. Times have changed – at least in the culinary sense – and eating seems to be a national pastime in Israel.

There is no definitive Israeli fare, just as there is no definitive Israeli. Rather, there is a unique merging of East and West, and the result is a profusion of culinary delights.

The predominant foodstyle, however, reflects the country's location – a mixture of Middle East and Mediterranean. So don't be led astray by restaurant signs offering 'oriental' food. In Israel, 'oriental' refers to the Middle East, and Oriental Jews are those of Sephardic (Spanish, Italian or Arab) heritage. Each Jewish ethnic group, whether Moroccan, Tunisian, Yemenite, Iraqi or native-born Israeli, has its own special dish and holiday fare.

A hearty breakfast

87

One principle holds Israel's multinational cuisine together: a practising Jew cooks and eats in a kosher manner. Only restaurants which can stand up to the strict eye of the rabbinical inspectors, the *Maschgiach*, are permitted to describe themselves as such. 'Kosher' means 'clean', 'pure' or 'permitted'. The rules upon which it is based are described as *kaschrut*. The Jewish cook learns from the Old Testament which ingredients and which methods of preparation are permitted. The three main rules of a kosher cuisine can be summarised as follows:

Firstly: 'Thou shalt not seethe a kid in his mother's milk' (Exodus 23, 19). Meat and milk may not be placed together in the same cooking pot, nor may they be brought together in the stomach after eating.

Secondly, it is forbidden to eat blood in any form, a prohibition which has an effect on the manner in which animals are slaughtered. The blood is allowed to run away completely, and offal, such as liver, is well salted to draw out the last drop of blood.

Thirdly, Jews are only permitted to eat mammals with cloven hoofs and ruminants, together with poultry and all sorts of fish which have scales and fins (Leviticus 11). This means that camel flesh and pork are forbidden, as are lobsters and shrimps.

Fruit and vegetable stall

The fish is fresh

In spite of these restrictions, the options are as varied as they are delicious. Visitors who do not wish to manage without cream sauces will find a number of hotels and restaurants which do not cook in the kosher manner.

Israel's cuisine differs from kosher food outside the country because the Arab influence makes the dishes

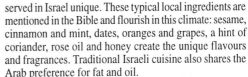

Bread stall

served in Israel unique. These typical local ingredients are mentioned in the Bible and flourish in this climate: sesame, cinnamon and mint, dates, oranges and grapes, a hint of coriander, rose oil and honey create the unique flavours and fragrances. Traditional Israeli cuisine also shares the Arab preference for fat and oil.

At midday, most people restrict their meal to a quick snack consisting of meat with various accompaniments. This may include *kebab* (beef and lamb), *shischlik* (grilled skewers of meat) and *shuarma* (pieces of mutton roasted in a spit). More elaborate menus are mostly served during the evening. The main meal often starts with salads and olives, seldom before 9pm; the hot day draws to a close with desserts, fruits and cheese.

Humus will be found on virtually every menu. The name covers various tasty purees of chick peas, onions and herbs. *Falafel* is the name given to fried chickpea balls; *boreka* are ravioli-like packets of dough with a spicy filling (cheese, spinach or potato). The popular *pita* bread pouches and stuffed aubergines known as *mashi* have also become popular in Europe, whilst *sahlab*, the sweet puree of orchids has not yet spread beyond the shores of the Promised Land. Visitors who like fish will fall for grilled John Dory (*mousht*) or marinated tuna (*palamida*), whilst those who prefer stews and casseroles will immediately take to *krupnik*, a mixture of pearl barley, beans, vegetables and meat.

Do try the fish, particularly in the seaside areas of Tiberias, Tel Aviv, Jaffa and Eilat. Trout, grey and red mullet, sea bass and St Peter's fish are generally served fried or grilled, sometimes accompanied by a piquant sauce. Authentic North African restaurants will also feature *harimeh*, hot and spicy cooked fish fragrant with garlic, tomatoes, cumin and hot pepper.

Sweetmeats

Israel is a paradise for those with a sweet tooth. Those unconcerned about their figures may well return home a few pounds heavier following the enjoyment of hazelnut cake (*baklava*), *konafa* with syrup and a variety of nuts, sweet rice pudding (*mahallebi*), *malabi* – a caramelised pudding – and candied fruit.

Eating out

Fruit juices (*miz*), milk (*chalav*) and other non-alcoholic drinks are available almost everywhere. Amongst the alcoholic ones, the most notable apart from the famous aniseed schnapps *arrak* are the wines (*yayin*). These have been produced for more than a century on the western slopes of Mount Carmel and in latter years also on the western slopes of the Golan Heights. The 'Rothschild' label is a sign of particularly good quality, and a bottle of red Cabernet Sauvignon or white Emerald Riesling will make a worthy accompaniment to any celebratory meal or farewell dinner.

Restaurant selection

Jerusalem (area code 02)

$$$ Alumah, Ya'avetz Street 8, tel: 6255014. Popular meeting place for health-food fans. **$$ El Marrakesh**, King David Street 4, tel: 6257577. Jews from Morocco prepare their specialities. **$ Ocean**, Rivlin Street 7, tel: 6247501. Elegant fish restaurant with first-class selections.

Tel Aviv/Jaffa (area code 03)

$$ Taboon, Yehuda Hayamit Street, in the Jaffa district, tel: 6816011. Very good fish restaurant near the port; outdoor dining available. **$$ Picasso**, Hayarkon Street 88, corner of Bograshov Street, tel: 5102784. Fashionable café with sea view; cheap breakfasts; open 24 hours. **$ Rive**, Sixty Street 118, in the southern part of Jaffa, tel: 595685. Large, friendly restaurant open until late.

Eilat (area code 07)

$$ La Boheme, Coral Beach, tel: 6374222. Elegant fish restaurant. **$$ The Last Refuge**, Coral Beach, tel: 6372437. The most famous fish restaurant in town.

Haifa (area code 04)

$$ Neptun, Pinhas Margolin St, tel: 8522654. Pleasant fish restaurant by the sea.

Restaurant sign, Tiberias

Tiberias (area code 06)

Along the lakeshore promenade there are plenty of good fish restaurants with a view across the Sea of Galilee towards Golan. Particularly recommended is **$$ Nof Kinnaret**, with a pretty garden, tel: 6790249.

Herzliya (area code 09)

$$ Taverna (in the Hotel Sharon), Ramat Yam Street, tel: 9575777. Large restaurant with sea view.

Netanya (area code 09)

$$ Los Troncos, Nice Boulevard 12, tel: 8617660. Excellent steaks.

Caesarea (area code 06)

$$$ Caesar (in the Hotel Dan Caesarea), tel: 6269111. Garden restaurant with a view of the golf course and pool.

Eating out, Old City wall, Acco

Acco (area code 04)

$$ Abu Christo, Yacht Harbour, tel: 9910065. Amid much competition, the Christo family still serves the best fish.

Beersheba (area code 07)

$$ Jade Palace, Histadrut Street 79, tel: 675375. Chinese delicacies in the middle of the desert; friendly atmosphere.

The undersea world of Eilat

Underwater observatory, Eilat

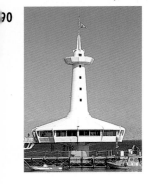

Active Holidays

Water sports

The Mediterranean shoreline and the Sea of Galilee are ideal for swimming, surfing, sailing and water skiing. The Tel Aviv marina offers yachting as well as sailing.

Skin and aqualung diving are especially popular along the Gulf of Eilat, where the season extends throughout the year. The area is usually free of large and strong waves; currents and tides are moderate, with variations of up to 80 cm (2½ ft) between high and low tides. These variations do not affect the diver's movement. Visibility is generally excellent, ranging from 15 to 40 metres (50–130 ft) and even more. Water temperatures range from 21°C (70°F) in February to 27°C (80°F) in August. A dozen diving schools serve the Red Sea. Prices are comparable to similar undertakings elsewhere in the world.

Apart from diving in the Red Sea, the Mediterranean also offers the possibility of combining diving with archaeological exploration. Underwater Roman ruins are amongst the destinations offered by the diving schools in Ahziv, Acco, Ashkelon and Caesarea.

The Mediterranean has two good diving seasons: autumn (September–December) and spring (March–May). Visibility on good days averages 10 metres (33 ft), with calm waters. Water temperatures range from 16°C (61°F) in February to 29°C (84°F) in August.

Contacts for skin and scuba diving equipment rental: Aqua Sport, Red Sea Diving Centre, Coral Beach, Eilat, tel: (07) 334404.

Federation of Underwater Activities in Israe, PO Box 6110, Tel Aviv Port, tel: (03) 457432.

Shikmona Diving Club, Kishon Port, Haifa, tel: (04) 8233908.

Basketball

Basketball fans should not miss the chance of attending a game. Few players can match the standards reached by this sport as Israel is as leading basketball nation.

Golf

The Caesarea Golf Club, 40 minutes by car from Tel Aviv or Haifa, welcomes tourists. The full-size 18-hole course is open all year and a driving range is available. Details: P.O. Box 1010, 30660 Caesarea, tel: (06) 361174.

Archaeology

Those who enjoy physical work and who also take an interest in archaeology can spend a day or several weeks assisting Jerusalem University in its excavations. Experience or background knowledge in archaeology are not necessary. The digs take place under expert supervision at a number of locations throughout the country. Go in search of Roman ruins in the Old Town of Jerusalem, for example, or look for remains from Biblical times at Hazor in Galilee. Those interested can apply each spring to obtain an up-to-date list of current archaeological projects, possible locations and work conditions.

Information concerning participation in excavations can be obtained from the Israel Antiquities Authority, PO Box 586, Jerusalem 91004, tel: (02) 5602627, 292628.

Kibbutzim

Voluntary work is also accepted in other spheres: young people up to 32 years of age can 'help out' in a kibbutz or a moshav at virtually any time. Food and accommodation are free, working clothes are provided and pocket money is often also included.

If you plan to work in a kibbutz, a minimum period of commitment is a precondition, usually at least four weeks. It is also necessary to submit a negative HIV test result with your application. The working week averages 36 hours (mostly 6 hours a day for six days). Travel costs are borne by the applicant.

Information on voluntary work in kibbutzim is available from: **United Kibbutz Movement**, Hayarkon Street 124, Tel Aviv 63432, tel: (03) 524 6156, 527 8874 (Sunday–Thursday 8am–2pm); **Kibbutz Arzi**, Leonardo da Vinci Street 13, Tel Aviv 64733, tel: (03) 435222; Kibbutz Hadati (religious kibbutzim), 7 Dubnov Street, Tel Aviv 64732, tel: (03) 695 7231 (Tuesday 12pm–4pm, Wednesday–Thursday 8.30am–4pm).

Information concerning work in a moshav can be obtained from: **Moshav Movement in Israel**, Leonardo da Vinci Street 19, Tel Aviv 64733, tel: (03) 695 8473 (Sunday to Thursday 8am–3pm).

An early kibbutz volunteer

Life on a kibbutz isn't all work

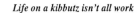

Getting There

By air

Ben-Gurion International Airport is situated in Lydda (Lod in Hebrew) near the Mediterranean coast, 20km (12 miles) southeast of Tel Aviv, 50km (30 miles) west of Jerusalem and 110km (68 miles) southeast of Haifa, and is the main hub for international air traffic. Its facilities include a Government Tourist Office, which is open around the clock to provide information and help arrange accommodation, tel: (03) 971 1485. General airport information can be found 24 hours at tel: (03) 971 2484.

About half the international flights in and out of Ben-Gurion International Airport are operated by the Israeli government-owned El Al Israel Airlines, which carries more than 2 million passengers a year. The airport is also served by many other major airlines, including British Airways and TWA. Eilat's temporary airport at Uvda is mostly used by charter aircraft.

Luggage checks are always very thorough. The Israelis do not rely on radar luggage checks but search all items by hand – one reason why El Al maintained such a good safety record in times of terrorist activity. It is therefore recommended that you arrive at the airport in good time (at least two hours before takeoff).

Signs are bilingual

Security is high-profile

By sea

Since 1993 it has also been possible to enter Israel by sea. Israel's main ports are Haifa and Ashdod. Official ports of entry for foreign yachts and boats also include Eilat and the Tel Aviv Marina. The Stability Line and Sol Line offer sailings from Europe to Haifa port, and many Mediterranean cruises include Israel in their itinerary. Between June and September the Arkadia Line operates sailings from Limassol (Cyprus), Rhodes and Piraeus to Haifa.

Overland

A 'green card' insurance certificate is required for cars temporarily imported into Israel. There are few border crossing points where one can enter Israel from the surrounding Arab countries. From Jordan, the main routes are via the Allenby Bridge near Jericho or the border crossing point at Eilat, which was opened in 1994. The Damiya Bridge, between Bet Shean and Nablus, has also been opened up to general traffic. For other points of entry from Jordan, check the latest details with Israel's Ministry of Tourism. From Egypt, one can enter the country along the common frontier on the Sinai Peninsula at Netafim, Nizzana and Taba. Near Rafiah there is a crossing point into the new autonomous region of the Gaza Strip, through which it is possible to continue overland to Israel.

Getting Around

94

Outside the airport

By air

Inland flights in small and medium-sized propeller aircraft can be booked through Arkia Airways (Tel Aviv, Dov Airport, tel: 03-426262). The airports served are Beersheba, Eilat, Haifa, Jerusalem, Rosh Pina (near Safed), Sodom (Dead Sea) and Tel Aviv.

By car

Driving in Israel is easy and convenient as the road network is comprehensive and well maintained. The only difficult aspect, as elsewhere in the world, is the parking situation in the town centres. Traffic regulations differ only minimally from those prevailing in Europe. It is advisable, however, to pay attention as infringements can result in a heavy fine. The main rules to remember are that speed limits are in general 40–50kph (25–31mph) in the built-up areas, 80kph (50mph) on country roads and 90kph (56mph) on motorways. Parking spaces are marked by blue-and-white pavement markings; prohibited parking by red-and-white ones. To assist orientation most road and information signs are written in three languages: Hebrew, Arabic and English.

Car rental is expensive

Car rental is relatively expensive, and fuel is not exactly cheap. Parking is restricted at all times of day and night. Cars, however, provide independence from public transport, which does not run from Friday afternoon until Saturday evening. The minimum age for renting a car is 21 years; a national driver's licence is sufficient if you aren't staying in the country for more than one year.

Public transport

Buses are infinitely superior to all other means of public transport, including trains. For this reason, every town has its own bus station (Central Station). Egged, the government-run bus company (Tel Aviv, Frishman Street 15, tel: 03-254271) runs timetabled services with its blue vehicles to almost all towns in the country and to Cairo. Tel Aviv is also served by the Dan bus service. All bus companies offer inexpensive rover and tour tickets.

A typical Tel Aviv jam

Israel also offers an unusual form of transport for short distances: a synthesis between taxi and bus. Sherut taxis are multiple-occupancy taxis which run along specific routes and which do not set out until all seats have been taken. Depending upon the distance travelled, each passenger contributes to the cost.

Train station, Haifa

Compared with the comprehensive network served by the buses and multiple-occupancy taxis, the train link between Tel Aviv and Nahariya-Haifa seems very modest (Israel Railways, PO Box 44, Haifa, tel: 04-856 4154).

Facts for the Visitor

Visas

The only requirement for entry is a passport valid for at least six months. Tourists are permitted to stay for up to three months in Israel without further formalities. For longer periods the Ministry of the Interior readily grants residence permits.

If you want to continue your journey from Israel through an Arab country, you should insist that your date of entry into Israel is not stamped into your passport but on a separate form. With the exception of Egypt and Jordan, most Arab countries refuse entry to tourists who have visited Israel. Should you wish to travel on to Egypt or Jordan, make sure you obtain a visa in advance from the embassy in Tel Aviv. Visas for southern Sinai can be obtained in Taba.

Decisions, decisions...

Customs

Apart from items for personal use, visitors may import duty free one litre of spirits, up to two litres of wine, 250 cigarettes, 250ml perfume, 10 films and gifts to a total value of US$125. Items such as video recorders of all kinds, computers or diving equipment must be declared. If these are intended for personal use, no duty will be charged but a deposit linked to the value of the goods in question must be paid.

Tourist Information

In the UK: Israel Government Tourist Office, 18 Great Marlborough Street, London W1V 1AF, tel: (0171) 299 1111.

In the US: 19th Floor, Empire State Building, 350 Fifth Avenue, New York, NY 10118, tel: (212) 560 0600.

Tourist information offices in Israel

Jerusalem: Rehov King George 24, tel: (02) 675 4906; Jaffa Gate, tel: (02) 628 2295; Pilgrim and Christian Tourist Office, Omar Ibn el-Khattab Square, behind the Jaffa Gate, tel: (02) 628 7647, 628 0382.

Tel Aviv-Jaffa: Central Bus Station, tel: (03) 639 5660.

Eilat: Khan Amiel Centre, Ofir Park, tel: (07) 633 4352.

Haifa: Herzl Blvd 18, tel: (04) 866 6521.

Tiberias: Habanim Street 23, tel: (06) 672 5666.

Acco: El Jazzar-Street (opposite the mosque), tel: (04) 911764.

Currency and exchange

The shekel (more precisely, the New Israel Shekel, abbreviated to NIS) and the Agorot (1 shekel = 100 Agorot) are the official units of currency.

Keying for cash

There is no limit to the amounts of foreign currencies which may be imported, but Israeli shekels may be imported up to a maximum value of only US$500. In view of the currency losses resulting from the considerably less favourable exchange rate offered outside Israel, it is unwise to export shekels. Before leaving the country, however, only a maximum, again, of the equivalent of US$500 may be changed back into foreign currency without a receipt. If receipts are presented, however, unlimited amounts of NIS can be changed. The moral: keep currency receipts.

Credit cards are widely used and accepted. Traveller's cheques will also be accepted without difficulty.

Foreign currency can be changed in any bank and at the specially designated bureaux de change, as well as in most hotels.

Tipping

There are two attitudes to tipping in Israel. Firstly an appropriate tip (according to European standards – approximately 10 percent) is given for good service. Included in this category is the obligatory tip for porters (approx. US$1 per piece of luggage). The second variation is that based on the Arab tradition: guests hoping for particularly friendly service during their stay offer the tip upon arrival, thus opening up the prospect of an equally high tip upon departure. Sherut taxis are not tipped; cab drivers don't need to be, but it will be appreciated.

Old-style shopping

Opening times

All shops and institutions are closed during the Sabbath (Friday afternoon until Saturday evening).

Normal Business Hours: Sunday to Thursday 8.30am–1pm and 4pm–7pm, Friday and public holidays 9am–1pm. Bazaars close at dusk; department stores are open all day.

Banks: Sunday to Thursday 8.30am–12 noon and 4pm–5.30pm; Monday, Wednesday and Friday: mornings only.

Official bodies: Sunday to Thursday 8am–12 noon.

Newspapers

Most newspapers are written in Hebrew, including the *Maariv* and *Haarnetz*. The English-language daily newspaper *Jerusalem Post* and the weekly magazine *Jerusalem Report* are amongst the most reliable sources of information in the country.

Postal services

All post offices are open Sunday to Thursday 8am–12.30pm and 3.30pm–6.30pm (except Wednesday afternoon). On Friday, the eve of the Sabbath and on the eve of other public holidays, post offices are only open between

8am and noon. They remain closed on Saturday. From Sunday to Thursday only the main post offices in Jerusalem, Tel Aviv and Haifa are open all day between 7am and 7pm.

Telephone

Have card, will talk

To make telephone calls within Israel it is necessary to purchase a telephone card (Telecard). Telecards to the value of 11.50 NIS (30 units), 26 NIS (50 units) and 58 NIS (120 units) can be purchased in post offices, kiosks and the larger hotels.

The rates charged by hotels for international calls are high, so it is therefore advisable to use a public card phone or to go to a *Bezeq Telephone Office* (Sunday to Thursday 8am–9pm, Friday 8am–1pm).

The dialling code for England from Israel is 0044; for the US and Canada it is 001. The country code for calling Israel from England is 00 972.

US phone card access numbers include: AT&T 177-100-2727; MCI 177-150-2727; Sprint 177-102-2727.

Radio

The Israeli Radio programme Kol Israel broadcasts the news in English daily at 7am, 1pm, 5pm and 8pm and in French at 7.15am, 1.30pm and 8pm (Medium Wave, 576 and 1458 kHz).

Time

Read all about it

Israel uses Eastern European Time, which is two hours ahead of GMT and seven hours ahead of Eastern Standard Time in the US. Israeli Summer Time begins in March and ends in September. However, the dates are not exactly the same as in Europe.

Voltage

220V alternating current. Adaptors for the mostly three-prong power sockets can be purchased in Israel.

Units of measurement

Israel uses the metric system. The sizes of clothing and shoes in the shops correspond in general to those used in Continental Europe. Expensive clothing is often sized according to the American system.

Value Added Tax

Value Added Tax (VAT) is at present 17 percent. It is often omitted from prices quoted and must therefore be added to obtain the total sum. No VAT is payable on hotel bills , car rental charges or air tickets if these are paid in foreign currency. If goods are exported the VAT can be reimbursed at the airport.

Picking a precious stone

Souvenirs

For visitors wishing to buy expensive souvenirs, diamond jewellery and tailor-made smoking and leather goods may be purchased free of tax and customs duties. Also typical, but less expensive, are wines from Mount Carmel, pieces of salt from the Dead Sea, olive branches and oriental spices.

Photography

Visitors to Israel should take plenty of replacement films with them, as they are considerably more expensive there. Because of the harsh light, a UV filter is recommended. Care should be exercised when entering and leaving the country: cameras are often opened, so it is advisable not to insert a film beforehand, or to remove it from your camera in good time.

There are no legal restrictions on photography; however, it is only polite to avoid taking photos of devout Jews on the Sabbath.

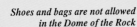
Shoes and bags are not allowed in the Dome of the Rock

Etiquette

After receiving some service or purchase, it is polite to say *toda* (thanks) or *toda raba* (thanks very much). Often the response will be *bevakasha* (please) or *alo davar* (it's nothing). The standard hello or goodbye is *shalom* (peace). 'See you' is *lehitra'ot*.

Dress

During the hot, dry season from April to October, light summer clothing is sufficient, although a warm pullover is recommended for the evenings and trips to the mountains. Stout footwear is advisable for those planning to undertake lengthy sightseeing tours. Between November and March it can be cool and wet, so visitors should also pack a warm coat or a jacket as well as a raincoat.

Casual or sporting dress is the norml; 'overdressed' visitors will feel out of place. In orthodox homes men should wear a hat and women a headscarf.

Nude bathing

Nude bathing is prohibited. Topless bathing is generally frowned upon.

Medical

First aid is available at any time from the Israeli version of the Red Cross, the Magen David Adom ('Red Star of David'), tel: 101 (throughout the country).

Medical out-patient treatment is available in all larger towns; it can be obtained via the following telephone numbers: Haifa, tel: (04) 522222; Jerusalem, tel: (02) 423133; Tel Aviv, tel: (03) 546 0111.

On guard outside the Church of the Nativity

Emergencies
Police, tel: 100 (nationwide)
Fire Brigade, tel: 102 (nationwide)
Ambulance/ First Aid, tel: 101 (nationwide)
Breakdown Assistance: MEMSI (Automobile Club), tel: (03) 561 3760

Vaccinations
There are no official vaccination requirements. Protection against tetanus is advisable.

Handicapped visitors
Israel provides excellent facilities for the handicapped. Many coaches and hotels are equipped to cope with wheelchairs, interpreters are available to translate sign language for deaf and dumb visitors, and during tours for blind holidaymakers arrangements can be made for display cases in museums and excavation sites to be opened to enable them to touch the exhibits.

Information can be obtained from the Milbat Advisory Centre at the Sheba Medical Centre in Tel Aviv, tel: (03) 530 3739. Wheelchairs and other forms of transport such as crutches can be hired free of charge from the Organisation Yad Sarah in Jerusalem, tel: (02) 6244242.

Health insurance
Israeli doctors prefer foreign patients to settle their bills immediately. Holiday health insurance is recommended.

Diplomatic representation
United States of America: 71 Rehov Hayarkon, 63903 Tel Aviv, tel: (03) 517 4338.
Great Britain: 192 Rehov Hayarkon, 63405 Tel Aviv, tel: (03) 524 9171.

No dogs or tennis

Travelling light

Hotels along Tel Aviv's coast

Accommodation

Israel is a place where Occident and Orient meet head-on, a fact reflected in the accommodation available. There more than 350 hotels of varying standards, including those of the big international chains. Jerusalem alone can boast 80 Jewish and more than a dozen Arab hotels offering accommodation to suit almost every pocket. Visitors can judge a hotel by the number of stars (five represent the highest category), but there is no legal guarantee of reliability. The IHA produces an up-to-date survey of all hotels (IHA, Hamered Street 29, PO Box 50066, Tel Aviv, tel: (03) 517 0131, fax: 510 0197.

It is unwise to travel without confirmed reservations, especially during public holiday periods. Hotel prices correspond roughly with those in England and the US. Double rooms are not significantly more expensive than single ones as a double is usually provided for single occupancy. Prices are 20–25 percent higher during the main season from July to August and on Jewish or Christian holidays. During the low season (mid-November until the end of February) discounts of up to 30 percent may be had. You must add to quoted prices 17 percent value-added tax if the account is settled in shekels, plus a 10 percent service charge unless this is included in the basic room rate.

In addition, Israel can offer more than 30 youth hostels of varying sizes (US$12–16 a night). Some are housed in traditional buildings, so that visitors may be swept into an Oriental-European atmosphere as in the youth hostel in Acco. As elsewhere, however, some Israeli youth hostels are no more than vast dormitories.

A complete register of youth hostels is available from the Israel Youth Hostels Association, Dorot Rishonim Street 3, PO Box 1075, 91009 Jerusalem, tel: (02) 625 2706, 625 0880, which also publishes colour brochures describing inexpensive routes (*Israel on the Youth Trail*).

Apart from these state-run youth hostels there are also small privately-operated boarding houses which also describe themselves as youth hostels. Most are less comfortable than the state-run establishments.

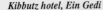

Kibbutz hotel, Ein Gedi

In the vicinity of the main places of pilgrimage, religious denominations have established Christian boarding houses with priority booking for pilgrims. A list is available from the Israel Tourism Administration, Pilgrimage Division, PO Box 1018, Jerusalem; tel: (02) 624 1281. The Lutheran Church in Bethlehem runs a cultural centre which not only accommodates visitors but is also a meeting place and peace centre. It also provides names of establishments in other Palestinian towns. Visitors can also contact the International Center of Bethlehem, PO Box 162, Bethlehem, West Bank, tel: (02) 647 0047, fax: (02) 647 0048.

However, those seeking a 'typically Israeli' experience may prefer to stay in one of the country's 25 kibbutz hotels. These superior hotels lie away from the bustle of the towns; they are run by the inhabitants of a kibbutz and make a valuable contribution to the economic viability of the community. Contact the Kibbutz Hotels Reservation Centre, 90 Ben Yehuda Street, 61031 Tel Aviv, tel: (03) 524 6161. This association also provides information on tours organised by Kibbutz Hotels. Inexpensive excursions are run even to remote parts of the country.

For visitors wishing to sleep under the stars: camping outside the official sites is strictly forbidden. There are 16 campsites with good facilities and round-the-clock security. Information can be obtained from: Israel Camping Association, Meshek 112, 50297 Mishmar Hashiva, tel: (03) 960 4524, fax: (03) 960 4712.

Youth hostel, Jerusalem

Hotels

Hotels have been divided here into three price categories: $$$ = expensive; $$ = moderate; $ = cheap

Jerusalem (area code: 02)

$$$ **King David**, Rehov King David 23, tel: 620 8888, fax: 620 8882. Traditional luxury, the best of the best in a massive four-square hotel building. $$$ **American Colony Hotel**, Nablus Road, corner of Louis Vincent Street, tel: 627 9777, fax: 627 9779. Former city palace owned by a prosperous Turkish *effendi*. Located outside the Old City near the Damascus Gate. Retains its residential atmosphere thanks to Swiss management and top-rate Palestinian staff. The most attractive and interesting hotel in Jerusalem. $$ **Pontifical Institute Notre Dame of Jerusalem Centre**, Rehov Hativat Hatzanhanim, opposite the Old City near the New Gate, tel: 627 9111, fax: 627 1995. Large hotel owned by the Vatican. Impressive neoclassical building with oversized statue of the Virgin above the entrance. Favoured by well-to-do pilgrimage groups. $ **Mitzpeh Rachel**, Hotel in the Kibbutz Ramat Rachel, tel: 670 2555, fax: 673 3155. Spacious complex in the south of the city, ideal for families. $$ **YMCA - Three Arches**, Rehov King David 26, tel: 625 7111, fax: 623 5192. Quiet hotel in central location, its approach flanked by 12 cypress trees. Opposite the King David Hotel. Large rooms. $$ **Evangelical Lutheran Hospice**, Old City, St Mark's Road, tel: 628 2120. Attractive rooms with old arched ceilings.

King David Hotel

Bethlehem (area code: 02)

$$ **Bethlehem Star**, Al Baten Street, tel.: 743249, fax: 741494. Acceptable Arab-run establishment. $ **Franciscan Convent Pension**, Grotto Street, tel: 742441.

Tel Aviv/Jaffa (area code: 03)

The luxury hotels run by international chains are strung out along Hayarkon Street directly opposite the beach. The most northerly of these skyscraping hostelries is the Hilton (the most expensive and elegant hotel in the city). The cheaper hotels are mostly in the town centre; the youth hostel lies to the north, on the far side of the River Yarkon. **$$$ Hilton**, Independence Park, tel: 520 2222, fax: 527 2711. **$$$ Sheraton**, Hayarkon Street 115, tel: 521 1111, fax: 523 3322. Standardised luxury only five minutes from the town centre. **$$ Metropolitan**, Trumpeldor Street 11–15, tel: 519 2727, fax: 517 2626. Near the beach with a nice view of the city. **$ Shalom**, Hayarkon Street 216, tel: 524 3277, fax: 523 5895. Small hotel near the beach, not far from the Hilton. **$ Youth Hostel**, Bnei Dan Street 36, tel: 546 0719.

King Solomon's Palace

Eilat (area code: 07)

$$$ Club In, Coral Beach, tel: 638 5555, fax: 638 5533, Apartment hotel managed by Hilton, 200m from the beach. **$$$ Isrotel-King Solomon's Palace**, North Beach, tel: 633 4111, fax: 633 4189. 'Royal' luxury by the North Beach lagoon. **$$$ Elat Princess**, Taba Beach, tel: 636 5555, fax: 637 6333. Luxury hotel ideal for families with children directly on the beach near the Underwater Observatory. Run by the Perita group. **$$ Red Sea Sports Club Hotel**, Coral Beach, tel: 638 2222, fax: 638 2200. Comfortable sports hotel with large diving school. Directly on the beach. **$ Adi**, Tzofit on South Beach, tel: 637 6151, fax: 637 6154. Simple, but clean. **$ International Youth Hostel**, Derekh HaArava, tel: 637 0088. Large youth hostel on the southern edge of town, beside Sonesta Suites.

Haifa (area code: 04)

$$$ Dan Carmel, Hanassi Avenue 87, tel: 830 6211, fax: 838 7504. Understated luxury above the town with a view across Haifa Bay (specify a room on the north side). **$$$ Nof**, Hanassi Boulevard 101, tel: 835 4311, fax: 838 8810. Seven-storey glass-fronted high-rise with post-modern ambiance but personal atmosphere. **$$ Talpiot**, Herzl Street 61, tel: 867 3753. Small establishment in the centre of town on the edge of the Nordau pedestrian zone. **$$ Beit Oren**, Kibbutz hotel 8km (5 miles) southeast of Haifa on Mount Carmel. P.O.B. 701, Haifa, tel: 830 7200. **$ Carmel Youth Hostel,** HaMelekh Shelomo, tel: 853 1944. Large youth hostel in a suburb to the southeast, opposite the Sportan Country Club.

Carmel Jordan River Hotel

Tiberias (area code: 06)

$$$ Carmel Jordan River, Habanim Street, tel: 671 4444; fax: 672 2111. Largest luxury hotel in town (400 rooms).

Directly on the lake. **$$$ Radisson Moriah Plaza Tiberias**, Habanim Street, tel: 679 2233; fax: 679 2320. Large, comfortable hotel by the lake. Star-shaped high-rise architecture. **$$ Ron Beach**, Gdud Barak St, tel: 679 1350, fax: 679 1351. Apartment hotel directly on the north shore. **$ Tiberias Youth Hotel**, Hayarden Street, tel: 6721 775. Large youth hostel on the hillside near the lake.

Herzliya (area code: 09)
$$$ The Daniel, tel: 954 4444; fax: 954 46570. Fitness centre with all the trimmings. **$$$ Dan Accadia**, tel: 959 7070; fax: 959 7090. Holiday hotel with pleasant atmosphere. **$ Eshel Inn**, Ramat Yam Street, tel: 956 8208, fax: 956 8797. Two-storey building behind promenade.

Netanya (area code: 09)
$$$ The Seasons, Nice Boulevard, tel: 860 1555; fax: 862 3022. Luxury-class family hotel directly on the beach. **$$ Mercure Blue Bay**, Hamelachim Street 37, tel: 860 3603, fax: 833 7475. High-rise hotel above the beach. **$ Mitzpe Yam**, Karlibach 4, tel and fax: 862 3730. Small three-storey family-type establishment near the beach.

Caesarea (area code: 06)
$$$ Dan Caesarea, tel: 626 9111, fax: 626 9122. Golf hotel on the edge of a green oasis.

Acco (area code: 04)
$$ Argaman Sea Shore, tel: 991 6691, fax: 991 6690. Beach hotel on the road to Haifa. **$ Youth Hostel**, tel: 991 1982. Former sheikh's palace; in the Old City.

Where the young head in Acco

Safed (area code: 06)
$$ Rimon Inn, tel: 699 4666, fax: 692 0456. Picturesque location in the artists' quarter, private-house atmosphere. **$$ Ron**, Hativat Yiftah Street, tel: 697 2590, fax: 697 2363. Small hotel in the town centre, lovingly cared-for.

Ein Gedi (area code: 07)
$$ Ein Gedi Guest House, Kibbutz Inn En Gedi, tel: 659 4222, fax: 658 4328. Independent bungalows in an attractive park.

Mitzpe Ramon (area code: 07)
$$ Isrotel-Ramon Inn, tel: 658 8822, fax: 658 8151. High standard of comfort in the midst of the desert.

Beersheba (area code: 07)
$ Hanegev, Haatzmaut Street 26, tel: 627 7026. Small, clean hotel. **$ Youth Hostel**, Haatzmaut Street 79, tel: 627 7444. Large house in the centre of town.

Laundry service

Index